DANDY DICK

Arthur Wing Pinero

DANDY DICK

Adapted by Christopher Luscombe

OBERON BOOKS
LONDON
WWW.OBERONBOOKS.COM

First published in 2012 by Oberon Books Ltd
521 Caledonian Road, London N7 9RH

PB ISBN: 978-1-84943-423-2
Digital ISBN: 978-1-84943-526-0

Cover Illustration: Clive Francis
        Photography: Manuel Harlan
        Design: n9design.com

The music for this version of *Dandy Dick* was composed by Nigel Hess. Further details can be obtained from
Myra Music Ltd. / Bucks Music Ltd.
Email: splatz@bucksmusicgroup.co.uk
Tel: +44 (0) 207 221 4275

Introduction

S ir Arthur Wing Pinero occupies an intriguing position in the history of the British theatre. Since he was born in May 1855, halfway, as it were, between Oscar Wilde (born October 1854) and George Bernard Shaw (born July 1856), it's tempting to see him as the meat in the sandwich, a solid piece of the roast beef of Olde England between two Irish japesters. Yet Pinero came from Portuguese Jewish stock, and his ambition to become an integral member of the Victorian and Edwardian establishment may have had some connection with his outsider's background. In later life, he'd describe how, as an impoverished young clerk in a lawyer's office, he'd loiter outside the Garrick Club, watching the flow of the great men of the law, of literature and of the theatre come and go through its portals and promising himself that one day he'd be of their number. The drive to financial security and social standing achieved through popular success seems to have wielded a strong influence over Pinero's thinking. Posterity can judge too harshly if it suspects that a writer preferred fleeting commercial glory to lasting critical endorsement, and perhaps Pinero, the author of nearly 60 plays, has been unfairly sentenced in the dock of theatre history, compared with his great contemporaries Shaw and Wilde. *Dandy Dick* (1887) was the third of the 'court farces', named in honour of the Sloane Square venue where they were first seen, and they have, however, maintained his reputation, in addition to his backstage comedy, *Trelawny of the 'Wells'* (1898) and *The Second Mrs Tanqueray* (1893), a powerful indictment of society's attitude to women with a past.

Pinero's grandfather, Mark, was a highly successful lawyer, but the business he built up seems to have faded away under the ineffectual stewardship of his son John Daniel, the playwright's father. As a result, Pinero grew up in somewhat straitened circumstances, made all the harder to bear in view of the family's past prosperity. Perhaps these early years of genteel poverty sharpened Pinero's commercial instincts and made him determined not to follow his father's easy-going attitude to business. He seems to have been stagestruck from an early age and, after several years of office drudgery by day and amateur acting by night, he decided to turn professional. His first engagement took him in 1875 to the Theatre Royal in Edinburgh, where he was a useful, if not particularly gifted, member of the stock company. At this period, London stars would progress around the country, playing the roles which had made them famous with the resident company in support. Pinero then joined the company of the great actor-manager Sir Henry Irving, where even his usefulness was taxed when he was cast as Claudius to Irving's Hamlet, despite the considerable age-gap between them. He'd already taken a few stabs at writing when, in 1877, an SOS came from the management of the Globe Theatre, urgently seeking a short comedy as a curtain-raiser. Pinero supplied *£200 a Year* and the *Era* described how the curtain fell on the play "amidst hearty cheers, bestowed equally between Mr Pinero's little work and the performers".

It was *The Magistrate* (1885), the first of the court farces, that established Pinero as a playwright, confirmed by the equal success of *The Schoolmistress* (1886) and *Dandy Dick* (1887). Part of Pinero's achievement with these three plays was his rehabilitation of farce as a genre. In the eyes of the critical establishment, farce smacked of the lower entertainments which one could sample in the rough-and-ready theatres on London's periphery. In the elegant playhouses that were springing up all over the West End, audiences wished to see themselves reflected in events on the stage. Pinero grasped the fact that the public would experience a frisson of delight were they to see respectable people like themselves in danger of losing their social position because of some indiscretion. In the three court farces, we see representatives of the law, education and the church embroiled in farcical situations that threaten their position in the eyes of respectable society. In an interview at the time, Pinero stated that he had tried "to raise farce a little from the low pantomimic level" because "farce should have as substantial and reasonable a backbone as a serious play". Perhaps he is also making sport with characters who care too deeply about society's judgement because he senses such feelings in himself.

Not only did he realise his youthful ambition of membership of the Garrick Club within three months of the triumph of *Dandy Dick*, but he was also rewarded with a knighthood in 1909.

Pinero also played his part in the evolution of the hierarchy of the British theatre. Due to the enormous success of his plays, he demanded and was granted total control over his work by the actor-managers nominally in charge. In effect, he directed the plays by using methods that would hardly find favour today. An imposing if not intimidating figure with his shiny bald pate, heavy black eyebrows and glittering dark eyes, he would expect his actors to obey his every instruction on movement, on intonation and on line-readings. The actress Hilda Spong, who played Imogen in *Trelawny of the 'Wells'*, has left a vivid account of working with Pinero:

> "He gives you the voice, the style, the walk, the gesture, the heart and brain of the character. After that, he devotes three days to you exclusively, squeezes your innermost soul into the mould he wants… He insists upon scenery, properties and costumes being ready before he directs the play. Not a word is ever altered, not a word is ever added, the breath of life is in the manuscript and woe be he who alters a sigh, a smile, a tear in it."

In the introduction to a collection of Pinero's plays, J S Bratton considers one consequence of Pinero's method of directing:

> "In the hands of a writer, it [the style of working] was made to serve the preconceived text in a way that was new to the stage; it contributed, perhaps rather more than the plays themselves, to the transformation of British theatre around the turn of the 20th century, its appropriation by an intellectual elite."

In the view of most of the era's cultural commentators, the theatre had fallen on hard times, unworthy even to be regarded as an art form. According to William Archer, the critic and champion of Ibsen:

> "The British public wants sedatives and not stimulants in the theatre, and it is the essence of great and serious modern drama to be a stimulant and not a sedative."

Archer hoped that Pinero might play his part in the desired stimulation of the audience and *The Second Mrs Tanqueray* can be seen as the fulfilment of Archer's aspirations. Certainly the first-night audience at the St James's in May 1893 was in no doubt that they had witnessed a remarkable piece of serious work by the master of farce with an impassioned performance by Mrs Patrick Campbell in the title role. The *Evening Standard* hailed it as "a great play", while the critic Edmund Gosse approvingly quoted Ben Jonson when he argued that Pinero's achievement was "to raise the despised head of drama again, and strip her of those base and rotten rags wherewith the times have adulterated her form".

Shaw, of course, considered that he and not Pinero was the ideal candidate for such a task. In his review of *The Notorious Mrs Ebbsmith* (1895), which Pinero had written as a vehicle for Mrs Patrick Campbell, Shaw dismissed the play as "a piece of claptrap", condemning the playwright because "he has no idea beyond that of doing something daring and bringing down the house by running away from the consequences".

Pinero himself was well aware of the perennial tension between the instincts of the professional playwright and the demands of the creative artist. In a speech at a Royal Academy banquet in May 1895, he stated his position:

> "Whatever distinction the dramatist may attain in gaining the attention of the so-called select few, I believe that his finest task is that of giving back to the multitude their own thoughts and conceptions, illuminated, enlarged, and, if needful, purged, perfected, transfigured."

Whatever Pinero's lasting merits, *Dandy Dick* has held its place on the stage over the past 125 years. Perhaps best remembered is the 1973 Chichester production with Alastair Sim as the Dean and Patricia Routledge as Georgiana, which transferred to the Garrick Theatre in the West End in the same year. There have been two productions at the Lyric Theatre Hammersmith – the first in 1930, with Nigel Playfair and Marie Löhr, and the second in 1948, with design by Cecil Beaton and direction by Athene Seyler.

More recently, there have been touring productions – Michael Denison and Dulcie Gray played the leads in 1970, followed by Anthony Quayle and Margaret Courtenay in 1986. In the same year, Patricia Routledge revived her Georgiana for a radio version of the play with Alec McCowen as the Dean, while the 1935 film version starred the comic actor Will Hay, supported by a number of his comedy sidekicks.

Pinero died in November 1934, a somewhat neglected and marginalised figure. The inscription on his headstone reflects this melancholy state:

> "Forget not me among you
> What I did in my good time."

But the arrival of this new adaptation of *Dandy Dick*, along with a production of *The Second Mrs Tanqueray* due to be seen at Kingston's Rose Theatre in the autumn, makes one hope that perhaps Pinero's 'good time' has come again.

Al Senter

(A version of this article appeared in the programme for *Dandy Dick*.)

Adaptor's Note

Perhaps a short word of explanation is required for an adaptation of this kind. I have long been an admirer of Pinero, and was keen to direct one of his farces. I was surprised to find that *Dandy Dick* was out of print, but when I tracked down a copy I realised that although it contains vintage material, it was in need of editing for the farce to work for a modern audience.

We all know that comedy has a tendency to date, and although I would argue that *The Magistrate*, which preceded *Dandy Dick* by two years, hardly needs a word altering, the latter play has long passages which are hard to fathom nowadays. Of course, they're interesting to the theatre scholar, but comedy is a harsh business and I felt strongly that for the play to live today it needed to be shorn of the more obscure references.

The fact that we now prefer just one interval, and are apt to get restless if a play stretches much beyond a couple of hours, made a trim all the more desirable, and I hope that the version I've come up with is true to the original, while suiting modern tastes.

Pinero wrote *Dandy Dick* in Brighton in late 1886. He was clearly inspired by the local racecourse as well as by some local personalities (it's said that Noah Topping was based on a Brighton bobby), and the whole piece has a genial warmth that is in keeping with the famous seaside resort. In searching for a suitable play with which to launch Theatre Royal Brighton Productions, the rediscovery of this neglected classic seemed a happy choice. I'm extremely grateful to Howard Panter and all at ATG for the opportunity to present the play, to my splendid cast and production team, to Oberon Books for marking the occasion with this publication, and especially to my assistant director, Guy Unsworth, for his invaluable help with the text.

Christopher Luscombe
Brighton, June 2012

Characters

SALOME

SHEBA

BLORE

MAJOR TARVER

MR DARBEY

THE VERY REV. AUGUSTIN JEDD, D.D.

GEORGIANA TIDMAN

SIR TRISTRAM MARDON, BART

HATCHAM

HANNAH TOPPING

NOAH TOPPING

ACT I   Scene 1 – The Deanery (Morning)
               Scene 2 – The Same (Evening)

ACT II   Scene 1 – 'The Strong Box' (The Next Day)
               Scene 2 – The Deanery (A Few Hours Later)

St. Marvells, May 1887

This adaptation was first performed at the Theatre Royal Brighton, on 28 June 2012, produced by the Ambassador Theatre Group. It was the inaugural performance of Theatre Royal Brighton Productions.

SALOME	Florence Andrews
SHEBA	Jennifer Rhodes
BLORE	John Arthur
MAJOR TARVER	Peter Sandys-Clarke
MR DARBEY	Charles de Bromhead
THE VERY REV. AUGUSTIN JEDD, D.D.	Nicholas Le Prevost
GEORGIANA TIDMAN	Patricia Hodge
SIR TRISTRAM MARDON, BART	Michael Cochrane
HATCHAM	Michael Onslow
HANNAH TOPPING	Rachel Lumberg
NOAH TOPPING	Matt Weyland

Director, Christopher Luscombe
Designer, Janet Bird
Composer, Nigel Hess
Lighting Designer, Paul Pyant
Sound Designer, Gregory Clarke
Resident Director, Guy Unsworth
Dialect Coach, Martin McKellan

ACT ONE

The morning room of the Deanery in St. Marvells. There is a large arched opening leading to the library, and deeply-recessed French windows opening out to the garden. Another door leads to the hall. It is a bright spring morning, and an air of comfort and serenity pervades the place.

SALOME, a young woman of about twenty, is sitting with her elbows on her knees, staring into space. SHEBA, her younger sister, lies prostrate on the settee.

SALOME: Oh my, oh my, oh my!

SHEBA   Oh my gracious goodness, goodness gracious me!

SALOME: There's only one word for it – it's a fix.

SHEBA: It's worse than that – it's a scrape. How did you ever get led into it?

SALOME: How did *we* get led into it!

SHEBA: It was Major Tarver's proposal, and I believe, Salome, that it is to *you* Major Tarver is paying his attentions.

SALOME: The Fancy Dress Ball at Durnstone is promoted by *all* the Officers of the Hussars. I believe that the young gentleman you have impressed calls himself an officer, even though he is merely a lieutenant.

SHEBA: *(Indignantly.)* Mr. Darbey is *certainly* an officer.

SALOME: Very well then. When we appear tonight at the Durnstone Athenaeum, unknown to dear Papa, on the arms of Major Tarver and Mr Darbey, I consider that we shall be equally wicked. Oh, how can we be so wrong?

SHEBA: Well, we're not wrong yet. We're only *going* to be wrong; that's a very different matter.

SALOME: True. Besides, there's this to remember – we're inexperienced girls and have only dear Papa in all the world. And as for stealing out of the house when Papa has gone to bed, why, we're not old enough to know better. But oh, now that the ball is tonight, I repent, Sheba, I repent!

SHEBA: I shan't do that till tomorrow. But oh, how I shall repent tomorrow!

SALOME: *(Taking an envelope from her pocket.)* You'd repent now if you had seen the bill for the fancy dresses.

SHEBA: Has it come in?

SALOME: Yes, the Major enclosed it to me this morning.

SHEBA: Read it. Don't spare me!

SALOME: *(Reading.)* 'Debtor to Lewis Isaacs, *Costumier* to the Queen, Bow Street. One gown, shepherdess – period: late 18th century – fifteen guineas!'

SHEBA: Oh!

SALOME: 'Trimmings, linings, buttons, frillings – seven guineas!'

SHEBA: Agh!

SALOME: That's mine . . .

SHEBA: *(Putting her fingers in her ears.)* Now for mine – oh!

SALOME: 'One skirt and bodice – flower fairy – period indeterminate – ten guineas.'

SHEBA: Oh, rather less than yours . . .

SALOME: 'Trimmings, linings, buttons, frillings – five guineas! Wings – two guineas. Total – forty pounds, nineteen. Terms – cash!' *(They throw themselves into each other's arms.)* Oh, Sheba!

SHEBA: Oh, Salome! Are there forty pounds in the wide world?

SALOME: My heart weighs twenty. What shall we do?

SHEBA: If we were only a few years older I should suggest that we wrote nice notes to Papa and committed suicide.

SALOME: Brought up as we have been, that's out of the question!

SHEBA: Then let us be brave women and wear the dresses!

SALOME: Of course we'll do that – but the bill!

SHEBA: We must get dear Papa in a good humour and coax him to make us a present of the money.

SALOME: Poor dear Papa! He hasn't paid our *proper* dressmaker's bill yet, and I'm sure he's pressed for money.

SHEBA: But we can't help that when *we're* pressed for money!

SALOME: Suppose Papa refuses to give us a present?

SHEBA: Then we must play the piano very loudly when he's at work on his concordance.

SALOME: But don't let us wrong poor Papa in advance. Let us try to think instead how nice we shall look.

SHEBA: Oh yes – shan't I!

SALOME: Indeed, Sheba, and I shall too!

The butler, BLORE, enters from the garden.

BLORE: The two soldier gentlemen have just rode up, Miss Salome.

The girls clutch each other's hands.

SALOME: You mean Major Tarver?

SHEBA: And Mr Darbey? They must have called to inquire after poor Papa.

BLORE: Shall I show them in, Miss Sheba?

SHEBA: Yes, Blore, dear.

BLORE goes out.

SALOME: *(Checking her appearance.)* Am I right, Sheba?

SHEBA: Yes. Am *I*?

SALOME: Yes. *(Looking out of the window.)* Oh! Here they are! How well Gerald Tarver dismounts! Oh!

SHEBA: *(Seating herself in an artificial attitude.)* Where shall we be – here?

SALOME: *(Running to the piano.)* Yes, you be admiring my voice!

SHEBA: No, let's run out and then come in unconsciously.

SALOME: Yes – unconsciously.

They run off into the hall. BLORE shows in MAJOR TARVER and MR DARBEY, who are both in regimentals.

DARBEY: The Dean's out of the way, eh?

BLORE: Yes, sir, he is.

TARVER: Never mind – perhaps Miss Jedd is at home?

BLORE: Yes, sir, she is.

TARVER: It would be discourteous to run away without asking Miss Jedd after her father.

DARBEY: Deuced bad form!

BLORE: The ladies were here a minute ago.

SALOME and SHEBA walk in together. They stop in their tracks on seeing TARVER and DARBEY.

SALOME: Major Tarver!

SHEBA: Mr Darbey!

TARVER: *(Taking SALOME's hand.)* My dear Miss Jedd!

DARBEY: *(Taking SHEBA's hand.)* My dear Miss Jedd!

SALOME: You quite startled us.

TARVER: *(Apologetically.)* Oh, did we?

DARBEY: Awfully cut up to hear it.

SHEBA: You needn't wait, Blore.

BLORE: Thank you, Miss.

BLORE exits.

TARVER: We thought we'd ride over directly after parade to make the final arrangements for tonight. Have the costumes arrived?

SALOME: Yes, they came yesterday in a hamper labelled 'Miss Jedd, Secretary, Cast-off Clothing Distribution League'.

DARBEY: That was my idea – came to me in the middle of the night.

SHEBA: *(Thrilled with his ingenuity.)* Mr Darbey!

TARVER: Now, about this evening; at what time is the house entirely quiet?

SALOME: Papa goes round with Blore at half-past nine – after that all is rest and peacefulness.

TARVER: So, Darbey, if we're here with the closed carriage at ten . . .

SALOME: But suppose Papa should hear us crunching down the gravel path?

SHEBA: *(Looking out of the window.)* Oh, Salome! Papa!

SALOME: Papa?

TARVER: The Dean!

DARBEY: The Dean?

They all collect themselves in a fluster. The two girls go to meet their father, who enters from the garden. THE DEAN has a dignified demeanour and a noble brow surmounted by silver-grey hair.

SALOME: Papa!

SHEBA: Papsey!

On seeing his children THE DEAN *removes his hat and embraces them warmly.*

THE DEAN: Salome! Sheba!

SALOME: *(Taking his hat.)* Papa, Major Tarver and Mr Darbey have ridden over from Durnstone to ask how your cold is.

THE DEAN: Dear me! Major! Mr Garvey!

SHEBA: Darbey!

THE DEAN: Darbey! How good of you. *(With his girls still embracing him he extends a hand to each of the men.)* My cold is much better. But these inquiries strike me as being so kind that I insist – no, no, I *beg* that you will share our simple dinner tonight at six o'clock!

TARVER: Oh!

DARBEY: Oh!

THE DEAN: Let me see – Tuesday night is –

SALOME: Leg of mutton, Papa!

THE DEAN: Thank you. Mutton, hot.

SHEBA: And custards, Papsey.

THE DEAN: Thank you. Custards, cold. And a welcome – warm.

TARVER: *(Looking to SALOME.)* Well, I – ah *(SALOME nods her head to him.)* That is, certainly, Dean, certainly.

DARBEY: Delighted, my dear Dean – delighted!

THE DEAN, with an important cough, walks into the library and sits at his desk.

TARVER: *(In a undertone.) Now* what will happen?

SALOME: Why, don't you see, as you will have to drive over to dine, you will both be here, on the spot, ready to take us back to Durnstone?

DARBEY: Of course; when we're turned out we can hang about in the lane till you're ready.

TARVER: Yes, but when are *we* to make our preparations? It'll take me a long time to look like Charles the First!

SHEBA: We can drive about Durnstone while you dress.

SALOME: *(To TARVER, admiringly.)* Charles the First! Oh Major!

SHEBA: Shan't we all look magnificent?

TARVER: Grand idea – the whole thing!

They are all in a state of great excitement when THE DEAN re-enters, with an anxious look, carrying a bundle of papers.

SALOME: Here is Papa!

They rush to various seats, all in constrained attitudes.

TARVER: *(To THE DEAN.)* We waited to say good morning, sir.

THE DEAN: *(Taking his hand, abstractedly.)* How kind! Good morning!

DARBEY: Six o'clock sharp, sir?

THE DEAN: At six, punctually. Salome, Sheba, represent me by escorting these gentlemen to the gate.

SALOME, SHEBA, TARVER and DARBEY go out. THE DEAN sits on the settee, turning the papers over solemnly.

Bills! *(He rises, walks thoughtfully to a chair, sits and examines papers again.)* Bills! *(He rises again, walks to another chair, and sinks into it with a groan.)* Bills!

SALOME and SHEBA re-enter.

SALOME: *(To SHEBA, in a whisper.)* Papa's alone!

SHEBA: An admirable opportunity to ask for that little present of money.

They go across to THE DEAN and sit at his feet.

SALOME: Papa?

THE DEAN: Yes, my child?

SALOME: Have you any spare cash?

THE DEAN: Spare cash!

SHEBA: Pounds, shillings and pence, Papsey; or pounds, shillings, Papsey, and never mind the pence.

THE DEAN: Ha! ha! I am glad, really glad, children, that you have broken through a reserve which has existed on this point for at least a fortnight – and babbled for money.

SALOME & SHEBA: *(Laughing with delight.)* Ha! ha!

THE DEAN: It gives me the opportunity of meeting your demands with candour. Children, I have love for you, solicitude for you, but – I have no spare cash for anybody.

He rises and walks gloomily across to the piano, on the top of which he starts to arrange the bills.

SALOME: *(To herself.)* Lost!

SHEBA: *(To herself.)* Done for!

THE DEAN: And now you have so cheerily opened the subject, let me tell you with equal good humour *(Emphatically flourishing the bills.)* that this sort of thing must stop. Your dressmaker's bill is shocking; your milliner gives an analytical record of the feverish beatings of the hot pulse of fashion; your general draper blows a rancorous blast which would bring dismay to the stoutest heart. Let me for once peal out a deep paternal bass to your childish treble and say emphatically – I've had enough of it!

He paces up and down.

SALOME & SHEBA: Oh!

SHEBA: We've been brought up to be young ladies – that can't be done for nothing!

SALOME: Sheba may be small, but she cuts into a lot of material.

THE DEAN: My girls, it is such unbosomings as this which preserve the domestic unison of a family. Weep, howl, but listen. The total of these weeds which have sprung up in the beautiful garden of paternity is a hundred and fifty-six pounds, eighteen shillings and threepence. Now, all the money I can immediately command is considerably under five hundred pounds.

SALOME: Oh, Papa, what a lot!

THE DEAN: Hush! But read, Salome, read aloud this paragraph in *The Times* of yesterday. There, my child. *(He hands a copy of* The Times *to SALOME, pointing to a particular paragraph.)*

SALOME: *(Reading.)* 'A Munificent Offer. Dr. Jedd, the Dean of St. Marvells, whose anxiety for the preservation of the Minster Spire threatens to undermine his health, has subscribed the generous sum of one thousand pounds to the Restoration Fund.'

SHEBA: Oh! and we gasping for clothing!

THE DEAN: Read on, my child.

SALOME: *(Reading.)* 'On condition that seven other donors come forward, each with the like sum.' And will they?

THE DEAN: *(Anxiously.)* My darling, times are bad, but one never knows.

SHEBA: If they don't?

THE DEAN: Then you will have your new summer dresses as usual.

SALOME: But if they do? Speak, father!

THE DEAN: *(Gloomily.)* Then we will all rejoice!

SALOME & SHEBA: Rejoice?

THE DEAN: And retrench. The two Rs. Retrench and Rejoice.

The two girls cling to each other as BLORE comes in from the hall with two letters on a salver.

BLORE: The second post, sir – just in.

THE DEAN: *(Taking the letters.)* Thank you. Oh, Blore! This letter from 'The Sport and Relaxation Repression Guild' reminds me that tomorrow is the first day of the races – the St. Marvells Spring Meeting, as it is called.

BLORE: Indeed, sir? Fancy that.

THE DEAN: All our servants may not resemble you, Blore. Pray remind them in the kitchen and the stable of the rule of the house –

BLORE: No servant allowed to leave the Deanery, on any pretence, while the races is on.

THE DEAN: *(Kindly.)* While the races *are* on. Thank you, Blore. *(He opens the second letter.)*

BLORE: Thank *you*, sir. *(Aside.)* Oh, if the Dean only knew the good thing I could put him onto for the Durnstone Handicap! *(He goes out.)*

THE DEAN: Children! Salome! Sheba! Here is good news!

SALOME: *(Running to him.)* Good news?

SHEBA: What is it?

THE DEAN: Your aunt!

SHEBA: Left us some money?

THE DEAN: Your aunt is coming to live with us.

SHEBA: To what?

THE DEAN: To live with us!

SALOME: What aunt?

THE DEAN: My dear widowed sister, Georgiana Tidman. Good gracious! Georgiana and I reconciled after all these years! She will help us to keep the expenses down.

SALOME: Keep the expenses down?

THE DEAN: *(Embracing his daughters.)* A second mother to my girls. She will implant the precepts of retrenchment if their father cannot!

SALOME: But, Papa, who is Aunt What's-her-name?

THE DEAN: My dears – a mournful, miserable history! *(With his head bent he walks to a chair and holds out his hands to the girls, who go to him and kneel at his feet.)* When you were infants your Aunt Georgiana married an individual whose existence I felt it my sad duty never to recognise.

SHEBA: A bad man?

THE DEAN: He died ten years ago, and therefore we will say a misguided man. He was a person who bred horses to run in races for amusement combined with profit.

SALOME: How awful!

THE DEAN: Left a widow, you would think it natural that Georgiana Tidman would have flown to her brother, himself a widower. Not at all. Maddened, I hope, by grief, she continued the career of her misguided husband, and for years, to use her own terrible words, she was 'The Daisy of the Turf'.

SHEBA: What's that?

THE DEAN: I don't know. But at length retribution came. Ill luck fell upon her – her horses, stock, everything came under the hammer. That was my hour. 'Come to me', I wrote, 'my children yearn for you'.

SALOME & SHEBA: Oh!

THE DEAN: 'At the Deanery of St. Marvells, with the cares of a household, and a stable which contains only a thirteen-year-old pony, you may obtain rest and forgetfulness'. And she is coming!

SALOME & SHEBA: When?

THE DEAN: She merely says 'soon'.

SALOME & SHEBA: Ugh!

THE DEAN: Salome, Sheba, you will, I fear, find her a sad, broken creature, a weary fragment, a wave-tossed derelict.

Let it be your patient endeavour to win back a flickering smile to the wan features of this chastened widow.

BLORE enters with a telegram.

BLORE: A telegram, sir.

DEAN: A telegram, Blore?

THE DEAN opens the telegram.

SHEBA: No Aunt Tidman flickers a smile at me!

SALOME: I wouldn't be in her shoes for anything!

They grip hands earnestly.

THE DEAN: Good gracious! Bless me! Girls, your Aunt Georgiana slept at the Wheatsheaf last night, and is coming on here this morning!

SALOME & SHEBA: What?

THE DEAN: Blore, tell Willis to get the chaise out. *(BLORE hurries out into the garden.)* Salome, child, you and I will drive into Durnstone – we may be in time to bring your aunt over. My hat, Sheba! Quick! *(The clang of the gate bell is heard in the distance.)* The bell! *(Looking out of the window.)* No – yes – it can't be! Surely that isn't your Aunt Georgiana!

BLORE appears with a half-frightened, surprised look.

BLORE: Mrs Tidman.

GEORGIANA TIDMAN enters. She is a boisterous, jovial woman, sporting a billycock hat and coaching coat. The girls cling to each other; THE DEAN recoils. BLORE goes back into the garden.

GEORGIANA: Well, Gus, my boy, how are you?

THE DEAN: *(Shocked.)* Georgiana!

GEORGIANA: *(Patting THE DEAN's cheeks.)* You're looking a bit peaky, Augustin; they should give you a ten-miler daily in a blanket.

THE DEAN: *(With dignity.)* My dear sister!

GEORGIANA: Are these your two fillies? *(To SALOME.)* Kiss your aunt! *(She kisses SALOME with a good hearty smack.) (To SHEBA.)* Kiss your aunt! *(She embraces SHEBA, then stands between the two girls and surveys them critically, touching them alternately with the end of her cane.)* Lord bless you both! What names do you run under?

SALOME: I – I am Salome.

SHEBA: And I am Sheba.

GEORGIANA: Why, Sheba, your stable companion could give you a stone and still get her nose in front!

THE DEAN: Georgiana, I fear these poor innocents don't follow your well-intentioned but inappropriate illustrations.

GEORGIANA: Oh, we'll soon wake 'em up. Well, Augustin, my boy, it's nearly twenty years since you and I munched our corn together.

THE DEAN: Our estrangement has been painfully prolonged.

GEORGIANA: Since then we've both run many races, though we've never met in the same events. The world has ridden us both pretty hard at times, Gus, hasn't it? We've been punished and pulled and led down pretty often, but here we are *(Tapping him sharply in the chest with her cane.)*, sound in the wind yet. You're doing well, Gus, and they say you're going up the hill neck-and-neck with your Bishop. I've dropped out of it – the mares don't last, Gus – and it's good and kind of you to give me a dry stable and a clean litter.

SHEBA: *(In a whisper.)* Salome, I like Aunt, but she's not my idea of a weary fragment or a chastened widow.

THE DEAN: My dear Georgiana, I rejoice that you meet me in this affectionate spirit, and when – pardon me – when you have a little caught the *tone* of the Deanery –

GEORGIANA: Oh, I'll catch it; and if I don't the Deanery will a little catch *my* tone – it comes to the same thing.

SHEBA laughs.

THE DEAN: *(Reprovingly.)* Sheba!

GEORGIANA: Trust George Tidd to set things square in a palace or a puddle.

THE DEAN: George Tidd? Who is George Tidd?

GEORGIANA: I am George Tidd – that was my racing name. Ask after George Tidd at Newmarket – they'll tell you all about me. My colours were crimson and black diamonds. *(She produces her pocket handkerchief, which is crimson and black.)* There you are.

THE DEAN: Dear me! Very interesting! Georgiana, my dear. One moment, children. *(The girls go into the library.)* *(Tapping the handkerchief.)* I understood distinctly from your letter that all this was finally abandoned?

GEORGIANA: Yes – worse luck! They'll never see my colours at the post again!

THE DEAN: And the contemplation of sport generally – ?

GEORGIANA: I daresay you'll manage to wean me from that too, in time.

THE DEAN: In time? Well, but – Georgiana!

The gate bell is heard again.

GEORGIANA: There's a visitor. I'll tootle upstairs and have a groom down. *(Calling SALOME and SHEBA, who re-enter.)* Make the running, girls. At what time do we feed, Gus?

THE DEAN: Luncheon is at one o'clock.

GEORGIANA: Right. The air here is so fresh I shan't be sorry to get my nosebag on.

She marches out, accompanied by the girls.

THE DEAN: My sister, Georgiana – my widowed sister, Georgiana. Dear me, I am quite disturbed. Surely, surely the serene atmosphere of the Deanery will work a change. It must! It must! If not, what a grave mistake I have made.

(A thought strikes him.) Good gracious! No, no, I won't think of it! Still, it is a little unfortunate that poor Georgiana should arrive here on the very eve of these terrible races at St. Marvells.

BLORE enters with a card.

Who is it, Blore?

BLORE: Sir Tristram Mardon.

THE DEAN: *(Reading the card.)* 'Sir Tristram Mardon'. Dear, dear! Certainly, Blore, certainly. *(BLORE goes out.)* Why, Mardon and I haven't met since Oxford.

BLORE re-enters, showing in SIR TRISTRAM MARDON, a robust man with a ruddy face and cheerful manner – a thorough English sporting gentleman. BLORE goes out.

SIR TRISTRAM: Hullo, Jedd, how are you?

THE DEAN: My dear Mardon – are we boys again?

SIR TRISTRAM: Of course we are! Boys again! *(He hits THE DEAN violently in the chest.)*

THE DEAN: *(Breathing heavily – aside.)* I quite forgot how rough Mardon used to be. How it all comes back to me!

SIR TRISTRAM: Think I'm changed?

THE DEAN: Only in appearance.

SIR TRISTRAM: I'm still a bachelor – got terribly jilted by a woman years ago and have run in blinkers ever since. Can't be helped though, can it? *You're* married, aren't you?

THE DEAN: *(With dignity.)* I have been a widower for fifteen years.

SIR TRISTRAM: Oh Lord! Awfully sorry. *(Seizing THE DEAN's hand and squeezing it.)* Forgive me, old chap.

THE DEAN: *(Withdrawing his hand with pain.)* O-o-oh!

SIR TRISTRAM: I've re-opened an old wound – damned stupid of me!

THE DEAN: Hush, Mardon! Language!

SIR TRISTRAM: All right. What do you think I'm down here for?

THE DEAN: For the benefit of your health, Mardon?

SIR TRISTRAM: Ha! ha! Never had an ache in my life! And I've not come to hear you preach next Sunday either! No, I'm here for the races.

THE DEAN: The races? Hush, my dear Mardon, my girls –

SIR TRISTRAM: Girls? May I trot 'em into the paddock tomorrow?

THE DEAN: Thank you, no.

SIR TRISTRAM: Think it over. You've seen the list of starters for the Durnstone Handicap – ?

THE DEAN: No. I have not.

SIR TRISTRAM: No? Look here! *(Showing him a race card.)* Sir Tristram Mardon's Dandy Dick, nine stone two, Tom Gallawood up! What do you think of that?

THE DEAN: I don't think anything of it!

SIR TRISTRAM: *(Digging THE DEAN in the ribs.)* Look out for my colours – black and white, and a pink cap – first past the post tomorrow.

THE DEAN: Really, my dear Mardon –

SIR TRISTRAM: Good heavens, Jedd, they talk about Bonny Betsy –

THE DEAN: I grieve to hear it.

SIR TRISTRAM: *(Taking THE DEAN's arm and walking him about.)* Do you imagine, sir, for one moment, that Bonny Betsy, with a boy on her back, can get down that hill with those legs of hers?

THE DEAN: Another *horse*, I presume?

SIR TRISTRAM: No, a bay mare. George Tidd knew what she was about when she stuck with Dandy Dick to the very last.

THE DEAN: *(Aghast.)* George… Tidd?

SIR TRISTRAM: Georgiana Tidman. Dandy came out of her stable after she smashed.

THE DEAN: Bless me!

SIR TRISTRAM: Poor old George! I wonder what's become of her.

THE DEAN: My dear Mardon, I am of course heartily pleased to revive in this way our old acquaintance. I wish it were in my power to offer you the hospitality of the Deanery – but –

SIR TRISTRAM: Don't even think of it. My horse and I are over the way at The Swan. Come and have a look at Dandy Dick!

THE DEAN: Mardon, you don't understand. My position in St. Marvells –

SIR TRISTRAM: Oh, I see, Jedd. I beg your pardon. You mean that the colours you ride in don't show up well on the hill yonder, or in the stable of The Swan Inn.

THE DEAN: You must remember –

SIR TRISTRAM: I remember that in your young days you made the heaviest book on the Derby of any of our fellows.

THE DEAN: I always lost, Mardon; indeed I always lost!

SIR TRISTRAM: I remember that you once matched a mare of your own against another of Lord Beckslade's for fifty pounds! *(Shaking his head sorrowfully.)* Oh Jedd, Jedd – other times, other manners. *(Offering his hand to THE DEAN.)* Goodbye, old boy.

THE DEAN: You're not – you're not offended, Mardon?

SIR TRISTRAM: Offended? No – only sorry, Dean, damned sorry, to see a promising lad come to an end like this.

GEORGIANA enters with SALOME on one side and SHEBA on the other, apparently the best of friends.

By Jove! No! What – Tidd?

GEORGIANA: Hullo, Mardon!

They shake hands warmly.

SIR TRISTRAM: Of all the places in the world to find 'Mr. Tidd'! *(Roaring with laughter.)* Ho! ho!

GEORGIANA: *(Laughing.)* Ha! ha!

SIR TRISTRAM: Why, Dean, you've been chaffing me, have you?

THE DEAN: No!

SIR TRISTRAM: Yes you have – you've been roasting your old friend!

THE DEAN: *(With dignity.)* Mardon!

SIR TRISTRAM: Tidd's a pal of yours, eh? Ho! ho!

GEORGIANA: Ha! ha!

THE DEAN: Sir Tristram Mardon, Mrs Tidman is my sister.

SIR TRISTRAM: Your sister?

GEORGIANA: Yes, Mardon, that well-seasoned animal over there and this skittish creature come of the same stock and were foaled in the same stable. *(Pointing to SALOME and SHEBA.)* And there are a couple of yearlings here you don't know. My nieces – Salome and Sheba.

SIR TRISTRAM: *(To SALOME.)* How do you do? *(To SHEBA.)* How do you do? *(Heartily taking GEORGIANA's hand again.)* Well, I don't care whose sister you are, but I'm jolly glad to see you, George, my boy.

GEORGIANA: Gracious, Tris, don't squeeze my hand so!

THE DEAN: Children! I must speak to you. Excuse me, Mardon. *(Aside.)* Oh, what shall I do with my widowed sister? *(He goes into the garden.)*

SHEBA: *(To SALOME.)* That's so like Pa. Just as it was getting interesting.

They follow THE DEAN into the garden.

SIR TRISTRAM: Lord! How odd! You know your brother and I were at Oxford together, George?

GEORGIANA: Were you, Tris? Then are you putting up here?

SIR TRISTRAM: He won't have me.

GEORGIANA: Won't have you?

SIR TRISTRAM: Because I'm down here for the racing. You see, he's a Dean.

GEORGIANA: Is he? Well then, you can lay a thousand sovereigns to a gooseberry that in this house I'm a Dean too!

SIR TRISTRAM: I suppose he's thinking of the Canons – and the Bishop – and those chaps.

GEORGIANA: Lord bless your heart, they're all right when you cheer them up a bit! If I'm here till the Autumn Meeting you'll find me lunching on the hill, with the Canons marking my card and the dear old Bishop mixing the salad. So say the word, Tris – I'll make it all right with Augustin.

SIR TRISTRAM: No thanks, old fellow. The fact is I'm fixed at The Swan with – what do you think, George? – with Dandy Dick.

GEORGIANA: Oh! my old Dandy!

SIR TRISTRAM: I brought him down with me in lavender. You know he runs for the Durnstone Handicap tomorrow?

GEORGIANA: Know? There's precious little that horse does that I don't know, and what I don't know I dream. Is he fit?

SIR TRISTRAM: As a fiddle – shines like a mirror – not an ounce too much nor two little. He'll romp in!

GEORGIANA: He'll dance in! Tris, don't forget that Dandy Dick doesn't exactly belong to you – at least not *all* of him.

SIR TRISTRAM: No – I've only a half share. At your sale he was knocked down to John Fielder, the trainer. The other half belongs to John.

GEORGIANA: No it doesn't, it belongs to *me*!

SIR TRISTRAM: You!

GEORGIANA: Yes, directly I saw Dandy Dick marched out before the auctioneer I asked John to help me, and he did, like a Briton. For I can't live without horseflesh, if it's only a piece of cat's meat on a skewer. But when I condescended to keep company with the Canons and the Bishop here I promised Augustin that I wouldn't own anything on four legs. So John sold you half of Dandy, and I can swear I don't own a horse – and I don't – not a whole one. But half a horse is better than no horse, Tris – and so, we're partners.

SIR TRISTRAM: *(Roaring with laughter.)* Ho! ho! ha! ha! ha!

SALOME and SHEBA enter unperceived.

Ho! ho! – I beg your pardon, George – ha! ha! Well, now you know he's fit, of course you're going to back Dandy Dick for the Durnstone Handicap.

GEORGIANA: Back him? For every penny I've got in the world. That isn't much, but if I'm not a richer woman by a thousand pounds tomorrow night I shall have had a bad day.

SALOME: Oh, Sheba!

GEORGIANA: *(Spotting them.)* Hush! *(To the girls.)* Hallo!

SHEBA: It's only us, Aunt.

The girls go into the library.

SIR TRISTRAM: I'll be off.

GEORGIANA: Keep your eye on the old horse, Tristram.

SIR TRISTRAM: Never fear. Good morning, George!

GEORGIANA: Good morning, partner!

SIR TRISTRAM: Ho! Ho!

GEORGIANA: Ha! Ha! *(SIR TRISTRAM bursts out laughing again and GEORGIANA joins in.)* Oh, do be quiet!

GEORGIANA gives him a push and he goes out. SHEBA and SALOME immediately re-enter from the library.

Well, girls.

SHEBA: Aunt – dear Aunt –

GEORGIANA: Yes?

SALOME: Dear Aunt Georgiana – we heard you say something about a thousand pounds.

GEORGIANA: You've been listening?

SALOME: No – but we couldn't help hearing. And, oh, Aunt, a thousand pounds is such a lot, and we poor girls want such a little.

GEORGIANA: Money?

SALOME: Yes, we have rather got into debt.

GEORGIANA: Good gracious!

SHEBA: Oh, Aunt Tidman, Papa has told us that you have known troubles.

GEORGIANA: So I have – heaps of them.

SHEBA: Oh, I'm so glad. Because Salome and I are weary fragments too – we're everything awful but chastened widows. We owe forty pounds to Pa!

GEORGIANA: Why, you ought to be ashamed of yourselves, you girls!

SALOME & SHEBA: We are!

GEORGIANA: To cry and go on like this about forty pounds!

SHEBA: But we've only got fifteen and threepence of our own in the world! And, Aunt, you know something about the races, don't you?

GEORGIANA: Eh?

SHEBA: If you do, help two poor creatures win forty pounds, nineteen.

GEORGIANA: No, no! I won't hear of it!

SHEBA: Oh, do, do!

SALOME: Oh, do, do, do!

GEORGIANA: I won't. I say decidedly, I will not!

SALOME: Do, and we'll love you for ever and ever, Aunt Georgiana.

GEORGIANA: You will? *(She embraces them heartily.)* Bless your innocent little faces! Do you want to win forty pounds?

SALOME & SHEBA: Yes, yes!

GEORGIANA: Do you want to win *fifty* pounds?

SALOME & SHEBA: Oh yes, yes!

GEORGIANA: *(Taking her betting book from her pocket.)* Very well then, put your very petticoats on Dandy Dick!

The girls stand clutching their skirts, frightened.

SALOME & SHEBA: Oh!

Blackout.

SCENE TWO

After dinner. The fire and lamps have been lit. SHEBA is playing the piano, SALOME is lolling on the settee and GEORGIANA is pouring coffee.

GEORGIANA: Sugar, Salome?

SALOME: No, thanks, Aunt George.

GEORGIANA: Sheba?

SHEBA: No thanks, but one in the saucer to eat.

GEORGIANA: Quite a relief to shake off the gentlemen, isn't it?

SALOME: Do you think so, Aunt?

SHEBA: *I* don't think so.

GEORGIANA: H'm! Now I understand why my foot was always in the way under the dinner table.

She holds out two cups, which the girls take from her.

SALOME: I thought the dinner was an overwhelming success.

SHEBA: All our dinners are at the Deanery.

GEORGIANA: Awfully jolly. Mutton was overdone.

SALOME: That's our new cook's one failing.

GEORGIANA: But the potatoes weren't – they rattled.

SHEBA: Cook can never manage potatoes.

GEORGIANA: What was wrong with the custards?

SALOME: Well, it was cook's first attempt at custards.

GEORGIANA: However, they served one useful end. Now we *know* the chimney wants sweeping.

SALOME: But it was a frightfully jolly dinner – take it all round.

SHEBA: Yes, take it all round. One has to take things all round.

GEORGIANA: Major Tarver isn't a conversational cracker.

SHEBA: I fancy Mr Darbey was about to make a witty remark once.

GEORGIANA: Yes, and then the servant handed him a dish and he shied at it. So we lost that.

SALOME: Still, we ought to congratulate ourselves upon a –

GEORGIANA: Frightfully jolly dinner. *(Taking her betting-book from her pocket.)* If Dandy Dick hasn't fed better at The Swan than we have at the Deanery, he won't be in the first three. Excuse me, girls. I've some figures to work out. *(Reckoning.)* Let me see.

SALOME: *(Privately to SHEBA.)* All's settled, Sheba, isn't it?

SHEBA: Yes – everything. Directly the house is silent we let ourselves out of the front door.

SALOME: How do we get in again?

SHEBA: By that window. It has a patent safety fastening, so it can be opened with a hairpin.

SALOME: We're courageous girls, aren't we?

DARBEY: *(Off.)* I venture to differ with you, my dear Dean.

GEORGIANA: Here come the waxworks!

DARBEY and TARVER enter through the library, talking to THE DEAN.

DARBEY: I've just been putting the Dean right about a little army question, Mrs – Mrs – I didn't catch your name.

GEORGIANA: Don't try – you'll come out in spots. *(Turning to THE DEAN.)* Well, Gus, my boy, you seem out of condition.

THE DEAN: I'm rather anxious for the post to bring today's *Times*. You know I've offered a thousand pounds to our Restoration Fund.

GEORGIANA: What?

THE DEAN: Hush – I'll tell you.

He is about to do so when SHEBA speaks.

SHEBA: Mr Darbey has brought his violin!

DARBEY: *(Tuning up.)* Will you accompany me?

SHEBA: To the end of the world. *(She sits at the piano.)*

GEORGIANA: *(As DARBEY and SHEBA prepare to play.)* Well, Gus, my boy, you're not stabled in such a bad box after all! Here is a pure, simple, English Evening at home!

DARBEY plays and SHEBA accompanies him.

THE DEAN: *(Aside.)* A thousand pounds to the Restoration Fund and all those bills to settle – oh dear! oh dear! What shall I do?

SALOME: *(Aside.)* I hope my fancy dress will drive all the other women mad!

GEORGIANA: *(Aside, frowning at her betting-book.)* I think I shall hedge a bit over the Crumbleigh Stakes.

DARBEY: *(Aside, during a brief rest in the violin part.)* My mother says that my bowing is not unlike Joachim's. And she ought to know – she once heard him play.

TARVER: *(Aside.)* He always presumes with his confounded fiddle. I wish they'd ask me to sing. My tones have been compared to a beautiful bell.

SHEBA: *(Aside, as she plays.)* We must get Pa to bed early. Dear Papa's always so dreadfully in the way.

GEORGIANA: *(Aside.)* Oh! – there's nothing like it in any other country. A pure, simple, English Evening at home!

BLORE enters quickly, cutting The Times *with a paper knife.*

BLORE: The paper's just arrived, sir.

The music stops abruptly.

ALL: Blore!

THE DEAN: *(Taking the paper from BLORE.)* This is my fault – there may be something in *The Times* of special interest to me.

TARVER: *(Aside.)* Ha, ha! That's put paid to his encore!

THE DEAN: Thank you, Blore.

BLORE: Thank *you*, sir. *(He goes out.)*

THE DEAN: *(Scanning the paper.)* Oh! I can't believe it!

GEORGIANA: What's the matter?

SALOME & SHEBA: Papa?

TARVER & DARBEY: Dean?

THE DEAN: Children. Georgiana. Friends. My munificent offer has produced the desired result.

SALOME & SHEBA: Oh!

THE DEAN: Seven wealthy people, including three brewers, have come forward with a thousand pounds apiece in aid of the restoration of the Minster spire!

SALOME & SHEBA: *(Horrified.)* Ah!

GEORGIANA: Does that mean a cool thousand out of your pocket, Gus?

THE DEAN: Yes. *(Reading.)* 'The anxiety to which the Dean of St. Marvells has so long been a victim will now doubtless be relieved.' *(With his hand to his head.)* I suppose I shall feel the relief tomorrow.

GEORGIANA: What's wrong with the spire?

THE DEAN: It *is* a little out of repair – but not sufficiently to warrant the presumptuous interference of three brewers. Excuse me, I think I'll enjoy the fresh air for a moment.

He goes to the window and draws back the curtains – a bright red glare is seen in the sky.

Bless me! Look there!

LADIES: Oh! What's that?

THE DEAN: It's a conflagration!

SALOME: Where is it? *(Clinging to TARVER.)* Are we safe?

SHEBA: Where is it? *(Clinging to DARBEY.)* Are we safe?

THE DEAN: Where is it?

BLORE enters with a scared look.

(To BLORE.) Are we safe?

BLORE: The old Swan Inn's a-fire!

The gate-bell is heard ringing violently in the distance. BLORE returns to the hall. The young men and women rush out into the garden.

GEORGIANA: The Swan Inn? *(Madly.)* You girls, get me a hat and coat. Somebody fetch me a pair of boots.

THE DEAN: Where are you going?

GEORGIANA: To help clear the stables at The Swan!

THE DEAN: Remember what you are – my sister – a lady!

SIR TRISTRAM hurries in breathlessly. GEORGIANA runs to him.

SIR TRISTRAM: Oh!

GEORGIANA: Tris Mardon, speak!

SIR TRISTRAM: *(Exhausted.)* Oh!

GEORGIANA: The horse! The horse! You've got him out?

SIR TRISTRAM: Yes, safe and sound.

GEORGIANA: Safe and sound! *(She sinks into a chair.)*

SIR TRISTRAM: But George, his tail is singed a bit.

GEORGIANA: The less weight for him to carry tomorrow. *(Beginning to cry.)* Dear old Dandy, he never was much to look at.

SIR TRISTRAM: The worst of it is, the fools threw two pails of cold water over him to put it out.

GEORGIANA: Oh! that's done him! Where is the animal?

SIR TRISTRAM: My man Hatcham is running him up and down the lane here to try to get him warm again.

GEORGIANA: Where are you going to put the homeless beast up now?

SIR TRISTRAM: I don't know.

GEORGIANA: *(Jumping up.)* I do, though! Bring Dandy Dick into *our* stables!

THE DEAN: No, no!

SIR TRISTRAM: The very place!

THE DEAN: Georgiana, pray consider *me*!

GEORGIANA: So I will, when you've had two pails of water thrown over you.

THE DEAN: Mardon, I appeal to you!

SIR TRISTRAM: Oh, Dean, Dean, I'm ashamed of you!

GEORGIANA: *(To SIR TRISTRAM.)* Are you ready?

SIR TRISTRAM: *(Taking off his coat and throwing it over GEORGIANA's shoulders.)* George, you're a brick!

GEORGIANA: A brick, am I? *(Aside to him.)* One partner pulls Dandy out of The Swan – t'other one leads him into the Deanery. Quits, my lad!

They go out together through the garden.

THE DEAN: What is happening to me? It will be in all the newspapers. 'Dandy Dick Reflects Great Credit on Deanery Stables!' 'The Sporting Dean!'

He goes into the library and sinks into his chair, as the young men and women come in from watching the fire.

SHEBA: They're getting the flames under control.

TARVER: If I had had my galoshes with me, I could have been here, there and everywhere.

SHEBA: *(To TARVER and DARBEY.)* You had better go now; then we'll get the house quiet as soon as possible. Poor Papa looks worried.

SALOME: Poor Papa.

TARVER: We will wait with the carriage in the lane.

SALOME: Yes, yes. *(Calling.)* Papa, Major Tarver and Mr Darbey must go.

She rings the bell. THE DEAN comes in from the library.

THE DEAN: Dear me, I'm very remiss!

TARVER: *(Shaking hands.)* Most fascinating evening!

DARBEY: *(Shaking hands.)* Charming, my dear Dean.

BLORE enters.

SALOME: *(To BLORE.)* Major Tarver's carriage.

BLORE: At the front door, Miss Salome.

They all make their way out into the hall. As they go, DARBEY attempts to ingratiate himself further with THE DEAN.

DARBEY: Oh – and I say – let me know when you preach and I'll get some of our fellows to give their patronage!

SALOME: *(Calling to her father.)* Don't risk the cold, Papa!

GEORGIANA and SIR TRISTRAM enter from the garden.

GEORGIANA: Don't be down, Tris, my boy; cheer up, lad, he'll be fit yet, bar a chill. He knew me – he knew me when I kissed his dear old nose.

SIR TRISTRAM: He'd be a fool of a horse if he hadn't felt deuced flattered at that.

GEORGIANA: He's no fool. He knows he's in the Deanery too. Did you see him cast up his eyes and lay his ears back when I led him in?

SIR TRISTRAM: Oh, George, George, it's such a pity about his tail!

GEORGIANA: Not a bit of it. You watch his head tomorrow – that'll come in first.

HATCHAM, SIR TRISTRAM's groom, looks in at the French windows.

HATCHAM: Are you there, sir?

SIR TRISTRAM: What is it, Hatcham?

HATCHAM: I just ran round to tell you that Dandy's a-feedin' as steady as a baby with a bottle.

GEORGIANA: Don't close your eyes all night.

HATCHAM: Not me, mum. And I've got hold of the constable 'ere, Mr Topping – he's going to sit up with me, for company's sake.

SIR TRISTRAM: The constable?

HATCHAM: Yes, Sir Tristram. *(Coming forward mysteriously.)* Why, bless you and the lady, sir – supposing the fire at The Swan wasn't no accident!

GEORGIANA: Eh?

HATCHAM: Supposing it were insiderism – and supposing our horse was the object?

SIR TRISTRAM: Good gracious!

HATCHAM: That's why I ain't going to watch single-handed.

SIR TRISTRAM: Get back then – get back!

HATCHAM: Right, sir.

They go out through the garden as THE DEAN enters, followed by BLORE.

THE DEAN: *(Looking reproachfully at GEORGIANA.)* You have returned, Georgiana?

GEORGIANA: Yes, thank'ee.

THE DEAN: And that animal?

GEORGIANA: In our stables, safe and snug.

THE DEAN: *(With a groan.)* Oh!

GEORGIANA: You can sleep tonight with the happy consciousness of having sheltered the outcast.

THE DEAN: We're locking up now. The poor children, exhausted with the alarm, beg me to say goodnight for them. The fire is quite extinguished?

BLORE: *(Fastening the windows.)* Yes sir, but I hear they've just sent into Durnstone asking for the military to watch the ruins in case of another outbreak. It'll stop the wicked fancy dress Ball at the Athanaeum, it will.

SIR TRISTRAM: *(Returning.)* I suppose you want to see the last of me, Jedd.

THE DEAN: Mardon!

GEORGIANA: Where shall we stow the dear old chap, Gus, my boy?

THE DEAN: 'Where shall we stow the dear old chap?' I really don't know.

GEORGIANA: Let me see. We don't want to pitch you out of your loft if we can help it, Gus.

SIR TRISTRAM: No, no – we won't do that.

THE DEAN: I suppose there's always Sheba's little cot still standing in the old nursery.

SIR TRISTRAM: Just the thing for me – the old nursery.

GEORGIANA: Yes – but play with the toys quietly if you wake early.

THE DEAN: *(Looking round.)* Is there anyone *else* – before we lock up?

BLORE has drawn the curtains.

GEORGIANA: Put Sir Tristram to bed carefully in the nursery, Blore. He won't want rocking.

BLORE: Very good, mum.

SIR TRISTRAM: *(Grasping THE DEAN's hand.)* Good night, old boy. I'm too done in for a hand of piquet tonight.

THE DEAN: I never play cards.

SIR TRISTRAM: *(Slapping him on the back.)* Not to worry – I'll teach you during my stay.

THE DEAN: *(Aside, helplessly.)* Then he's *staying* with me!

SIR TRISTRAM: Good night, George.

GEORGIANA: Good night, old boy.

SIR TRISTRAM goes out with BLORE.

(Calling after him.) You may take your pipe with you, Tris! We smoke all over the Deanery.

THE DEAN: *(Aside.)* I never smoke. Does *she*?

GEORGIANA: *(Humming a tune merrily.)* Tra la, tra la! Now, Mr Tidd, we'll toddle. Tra la, tra la! *(She stops and looks at THE DEAN.)* Gus, I don't like your looks; I shall let the Vet see you in the morning. What's wrong with you?

THE DEAN shakes his head mournfully, and sinks onto the settee.

Money?

THE DEAN: There *are* bills, which, at a more convenient time, it will be my grateful duty to discharge.

GEORGIANA: And you're short?

THE DEAN: Short?

GEORGIANA: Stumped – out of coin – run low. What'll square the bills?

THE DEAN: Very little would settle the bills – but – but –

GEORGIANA: I know – the spire. Why, Gus, you haven't got that thousand?

THE DEAN: There is a very large number of worthy men who do not possess a thousand pounds. With that number I have the mournful pleasure of enrolling myself.

GEORGIANA: When's the settling day?

THE DEAN: Eh?

GEORGIANA: When will you have to fork out?

THE DEAN: Unless the restoration is immediately commenced the spire will certainly crumble.

GEORGIANA: Then it's a race between you and the spire which crumbles first. Gus, will you let your little sister lend you a hand?

THE DEAN: My dear Georgiana, impossible!

GEORGIANA: No, no – not out of my own pocket. Come here. *(She takes his arm and whispers in his ear.)* Can you squeeze a pair of ponies?

THE DEAN: Can I what?

GEORGIANA: Can you raise fifty pounds?

THE DEAN: Certainly. More than fifty pounds.

GEORGIANA: No – don't be rash! That's the worst of you beginners. Just fifty, by tomorrow morning.

THE DEAN: Most assuredly.

GEORGIANA: Very well then – clap it onto Dandy Dick!

THE DEAN: *(With horror.)* What?

GEORGIANA: He's a certainty – if those two buckets of water haven't put him off. There's nothing like him at the weight. Keep it dark, Gus – don't breathe a word to any of your Canons or Archdeacons, or they'll rush at it and shorten the price for us. Go in, Gus, my boy – take your poor widowed sister's tip, and sleep as peacefully as a blessed baby! *(She presses him warmly to her and kisses him.)*

THE DEAN: *(Extricating himself.)* Oh, Mrs Tidman! Go to your room!

GEORGIANA: Augustin!

THE DEAN: In the morning I will endeavour to frame some verbal expression of the horror with which I regard your proposal. For the present, you are my parents' child and I trust your bed is well aired.

GEORGIANA: Oh, very well, Augustin. I've done all I can for the spire. *Bon soir*, old boy!

THE DEAN: Good night.

GEORGIANA: If you're wiser in the morning just send Blore onto the course, and he can put the money on for you.

THE DEAN: Blore? My poor devoted old servant would be lost on a racecourse.

GEORGIANA: Would he? He was quite at home in Tattersall's Ring when I was at St. Marvells last summer.

THE DEAN: Blore?

GEORGIANA: Blore. I recognised the veteran sportsman the moment I arrived at the Deanery.

THE DEAN: What was my butler doing at St. Marvells Races?

GEORGIANA: Investing the savings of your cook and housemaid, I should think.

THE DEAN: Oh!

BLORE enters with his lantern.

BLORE: *(Beaming sweetly.)* I beg your pardon, sir, but shall I do the rounds?

THE DEAN gives BLORE a fierce look.

GEORGIANA: Blore.

BLORE: Mum?

GEORGIANA: Breakfast at nine, sharp. And pack a hamper with a cold chicken, some French rolls and two bottles of Heidsieck – label it 'George Tidd', and send it over to the Hill. Good night.

She goes out. THE DEAN sinks into a chair and clasps his forehead.

BLORE: *(To THE DEAN.)* A dear, high-spirited lady. *(Peering at THE DEAN.)* Aren't you well, sir?

THE DEAN: Serpent!

BLORE: Meaning *me*, sir?

THE DEAN: Lock up; I'll speak to you in the morning. Lock up. *(BLORE goes into the library, turns out the lamp there and exits.)* What dreadful wave threatens to engulf the Deanery? What has come to us in a few fatal hours? A horse of sporting tendencies contaminating my stables, his equally vicious owner nestling in the nursery – and my own widowed sister, in all probability, smoking a cigarette at her bedroom window with her feet on the window ledge! *(Listening.)* What's that? I thought I heard footsteps in the garden. I can see nothing – only the old spire standing out against the threatening sky. *(Leaving the window shudderingly.)* The spire! My principal creditor! My principal creditor and the most conspicuous object in the city!

BLORE re-enters with his lantern, carrying some banknotes in his hand.

BLORE: *(Laying the money on the table.)* I found these, sir, on your dressing table – they're banknotes, sir.

THE DEAN: *(Taking the notes.)* Thank you. I placed them there to pay into the bank tomorrow. *(Counting the notes.)* Ten, ten, twenty, five, five – fifty. Fifty pounds! The very sum Georgiana urged me to – oh! *(To BLORE, waving him away.)* Leave me – go to bed – go to bed – go to bed! *(BLORE is going.)* Blore!

BLORE: Sir.

THE DEAN: What made you tempt me with these at such a moment?

BLORE: Tempt you, sir? The window was open and I feared they might blow away.

THE DEAN: *(Catching him by the coat collar.)* Man, what were you doing at St. Marvells Races last summer?

BLORE: *(With a cry, falling to his knees.)* Oh sir! Oh sir! I knew that high-spirited lady would bring grief and sorrow to the peaceful, happy Deanery! Oh sir, I *have* done a little on my own account from time to time on the Hill, also on commission for the kitchen!

THE DEAN: I knew it! Get up, Blore – get up. Oh, Edward Blore, Edward Blore, what weak creatures we are!

BLORE: We are, sir – we are – 'specially when we've got a tip, sir. Think of the temptation of a tip, sir.

THE DEAN: I do, Blore – I do.

BLORE: I confess everything, sir. Bonny Betsy's bound to win the Handicap.

THE DEAN: No, no – she isn't.

BLORE: Yes she is, sir.

THE DEAN: No she isn't.

BLORE: Yes she is.

THE DEAN: No, she can never get down the hill with those legs of hers.

BLORE: She can, sir – what's to beat her?

THE DEAN: The horse in my stable – Dandy Dick!

BLORE: Dandy Dick? That old bit of mahogany, sir? They're laying ten to one against him.

THE DEAN: *(With hysterical eagerness.)* Are they? I'll take it! I'll take it!

BLORE: Lord love you, sir – how much?

THE DEAN: Fifty! There's the money. *(Impulsively he crams the notes into BLORE's hand and then recoils in horror.)* Oh! *(He sinks into a chair with a groan.)*

BLORE: *(Aside.)* Lord, who'd have thought the Dean was such an ardent sportsman at heart? He daren't give me my notice after this. *(To THE DEAN.)* Of course it's understood, sir, that we keep our weaknesses dark. Outwardly, sir, we remain respectable and, I hope, respected. *(Putting the notes in his pocket.)* I wish you good night, sir.

He walks to the door; THE DEAN makes an effort to recall him but fails.

(Aside.) And that man has been my pattern and example for twenty years! Oh, Edward Blore, your idol is shattered! *(Turning to THE DEAN.)* Good night, sir. May your dreams be calm and happy, and may you have a good run for your money!

BLORE goes out to the hall. THE DEAN gradually recovers his self-possession.

THE DEAN: I – I am upset tonight, Blore. Of course you leave this day month. I – I *(looking round.)* Blore? He's gone! If I don't call him back the spire may be richer tomorrow by five hundred pounds. I won't dwell on it. I'll read – I'll read. *(He goes into the library and snatches a book at random. There is the sound of falling rain and distant thunder.)* Rain, thunder. How it assimilates with the tempest of my mind! I'll read. *(He returns with the book.)* Bless me! This is very strange. '*The Horse and Its Ailments*, by John Cox, M.R.C.V.S.' It was with the aid of this volume that I used to tend my old mare at Oxford. A leaf turned down. 'Simple remedies for chills – the Bolus.' The helpless beast in my stable is suffering from a chill. Good gracious! If I allow Blore to risk my fifty pounds on Dandy Dick, surely it would be advisable to administer this bolus to the poor animal without delay. *(Hastily referring to the book.)* I have these drugs in my chest. There's not a moment to be lost! I shall want help. *(He goes to the bell and rings.)* I'll fetch my medicine chest.

He lays the book on the table and goes into the library. BLORE enters.

BLORE: *(Looking round.)* Where is he? The bell rang. The Dean's puzzling me with his uncommon behaviour, that he is.

THE DEAN comes from the library, carrying a large medicine chest. On encountering BLORE he starts and turns away his head, the picture of guilt.

THE DEAN: Blore, I feel it would be a humane act to administer to the poor, ignorant animal in my stable a simple bolus as a precaution against chill. I rely upon your aid and discretion in ministering to *any* guest in the Deanery.

BLORE: I see, sir – you ain't going to lose half a chance for tomorrow, sir – you're a knowing one, as the saying goes!

THE DEAN: *(Shrinking from BLORE with a groan.)* Oh!

He places the medicine chest on the table and takes up the book.

(Handing the book to BLORE with his finger on a page.) Fetch these humble but necessary articles from the kitchen – quick. I'll mix the bolus here.

BLORE: Very good, sir.

BLORE goes out quickly.

THE DEAN: It is exactly seven-and-twenty years since I last approached a horse medically.

He takes off his coat and lays it on a chair, then rolls his shirt sleeves up above his elbows and puts on his glasses.

I trust that this bolus will not give the animal an unfair advantage over his competitors. I don't desire that! I don't desire that! *(A flash of lightning.)*

BLORE re-enters pushing a trolley, on which are a small flour-barrel and rolling pin, a white china basin, a carafe of water, a napkin and the book.

Thank you.

THE DEAN: *(Reading.)* Three parts flour to one part water.

He mixes the bolus.

BLORE: *(Aside.)* His eyes are awful; I don't seem to know the happy Deanery when I see such proceedings a-going on at the dead of night.

There is a heavy roll of thunder. THE DEAN kneads the pudding.

THE DEAN: The old half-forgotten time returns to me. I am once again a promising youth at college.

BLORE: *(Aside.)* One would think by his looks that he was going to poison his family instead of – Poison? Poison! Oh, if anything serious happened to the animal in our stable there would be nothing in the way of Bonny Betsy, the deserving horse I've trusted with my hard-earned savings!

THE DEAN: I am walking once again in the old streets of Oxford, avoiding the shops where I owe my youthful bills. Bills! *(He kneads vigorously.)*

BLORE: *(Aside.)* Where's the stuff I got a month ago to dispatch the old black retriever that fell ill?

THE DEAN: Bills!

BLORE: *(Aside.)* The dog died – the poison's in my pantry – it couldn't have got used for cooking purposes.

THE DEAN: I see the broad meadows and the tall spire of the college – the spire! Oh, my whole life seems made up of Bills and Spires!

BLORE: *(Aside.)* I'll do it! I'll do it!

Unseen by THE DEAN, he steals out.

THE DEAN: Where are the drugs?

Opening the medicine chest and bending down over the bottles, he pours some drops from a bottle into the basin.

Chlorate of potash *(Counting.)* One – two – three – four. *(He replaces the bottle and takes another.)* How fortunate some animals are! Sweet spirits of nitre. *(Counting.)* One – two – three. It's done! It's done!

Taking up the medicine chest he goes with it into the library. As he disappears, BLORE re-enters, stealthily fingering a small paper packet.

BLORE: *(In a whisper.)* Strychnine! *(Forked lightning illuminates the room.)*

There is a heavy roll of thunder – BLORE darts to the table, empties the contents of the packet into the basin, and stirs vigorously with the rolling pin.

I've cooked Dandy Dick! I've cooked Dandy Dick! *(He moves away from the table in horror.)* Oh, I'm only an amateur sportsman and I can't afford uncertainty. *(As THE DEAN returns, BLORE starts up guiltily.)* Can I help you any more, sir?

THE DEAN: No, remove these dreadful things, and don't let me see you again tonight!

He sits with the basin on his knees, and proceeds to roll the paste.

BLORE: Good night, sir. *(He goes out.)*

THE DEAN: *(Putting on his coat.)* I don't contemplate my humane task with resignation. The stable is small, and if the animal is restive we shall be cramped for room. *(The rain is heard.)* I shall get a chill too. *(Seeing SIR TRISTRAM's coat and cap lying on the settee.)* I am sure Mardon will lend me this gladly. *(Putting on the coat, which completely envelops him.)* The animal may recognise the garment, and receive me with kindly feeling. *(Putting on the sealskin cap, which almost conceals his face.)* Ugh! Why do I feel this dreadful sinking at the heart? Put out the light! *(Taking the basin and turning out the lamp.)* Oh! if all followers of the veterinary science are as truly wretched as I am, what a noble band they must be!

The thunder rolls as he goes into the garden, shutting the curtains behind him. SIR TRISTRAM then enters quietly, smoking his pipe, and carrying a lighted candle.

SIR TRISTRAM: Ah! – fire still burning. *(Blowing out the candle.)* I shall doze here till daybreak. What a night! I never thought there was so much thunder in these small country places.

GEORGIANA, looking pale and agitated, and wearing a dressing gown, enters quickly, carrying an umbrella and a lighted candle.

GEORGIANA: *(Going to the window.)* This is the nearer way to the stable. I must satisfy myself – I must – I must!

SIR TRISTRAM: *(Rising suddenly.)* Hullo!

GEORGIANA: *(Shrieking with fright.)* Agh!

SIR TRISTRAM: Hush!

GEORGIANA: *(Holding out her umbrella.)* Stand where you are or I'll fire! *(Recognising SIR TRISTRAM.)* Tris!

SIR TRISTRAM: Why, George!

GEORGIANA: Oh Tris, I've been dreaming! *(Falling helplessly against SIR TRISTRAM, who deposits her in a chair.)* Oh! oh! oh! Don't look at me! I've overtrained. I shall be on my legs again in a minute.

She opens her umbrella and hides herself behind it, sobbing violently.

SIR TRISTRAM: *(Standing over the umbrella in great concern.)* My goodness, George! Whatever shall I do? Shall I trot you up and down outside?

GEORGIANA: Be quiet! *(Sobbing.)* What are you fooling about down here for? Why can't you lie quietly in your cot?

SIR TRISTRAM: Confound that cot! Why, it wouldn't hold my photograph. Where were *you* going?

GEORGIANA: Into the stable to sit with Dandy. The thunder's awful in my room; when it gets tired it seems to sit down on my particular bit of roof. I did doze once, and then I had a frightful dream. I dreamt that Dandy had been sold to the circus, and that they were hooting at him because he had lost his tail. There's an omen!

SIR TRISTRAM: Don't, don't – be a man, George, be a man!

GEORGIANA: *(Shutting her umbrella.)* You're right – I'm dreadfully effeminate. There – Tidd's herself again!

SIR TRISTRAM: Bravo! Come along!

Turning towards the window, he suddenly stops and looks at her, and then seizes her hand. Eventually, he speaks.

George, you've robbed me tonight of an old pal.

GEORGIANA: I? What d'ye mean?

SIR TRISTRAM: I mean that I seem to have dropped the acquaintance of George Tidd, Esquire, and gained an introduction to his twin sister, Georgiana.

GEORGIANA: Oh, don't be so soft, man. Stay where you are; I'll nurse Dandy on my own. *(She goes towards the window, then starts back.)* Hush!

SIR TRISTRAM: What's the matter?

GEORGIANA: Didn't you hear something?

SIR TRISTRAM: Where?

GEORGIANA: *(Pointing to the window.)* There.

SIR TRISTRAM: *(Peeping through the curtains.)* You're right. Some people moving about the garden.

GEORGIANA: Tris! The horse!

SIR TRISTRAM: They're not near the stables. They're coming in here. Hush! We'll clear out and watch!

SIR TRISTRAM takes the candlestick and they go into the library, leaving the room in darkness. The curtains at the window are pushed aside, and SALOME and SHEBA enter; both are in fancy dress.

SALOME: *(In a rage.)* Oh! oh! oh!

SHEBA: No ball after all!

SALOME: If only we had a brother to avenge us!

SHEBA: I shall try and borrow a brother tomorrow!

SALOME: Cold, wretched, splashed and in debt – for nothing!

SHEBA: To think that we've had all the inconvenience of being wicked and rebellious and have only half done it!

SALOME: This comes of stooping to the Military!

SHEBA: It serves us right – we've been trained as clergy wives. I hate Nugent Darbey – I hope he grows bald early!

SALOME: Gerald Tarver's nose is inclined to pink – may it deepen and deepen till it frightens cows!

Voices are heard outside.

DARBEY: Miss Jedd – Sheba!

TARVER: Pray hear two wretched men! Miss Jedd!

SALOME: *(In a whisper.)* There they are.

SHEBA: Shall we grant them a dignified interview?

SALOME: Yes. Curl your lip, Sheba.

SHEBA: Your lip curls better than mine – I'll dilate my nostrils.

> *SALOME draws aside the curtains and TARVER and DARBEY enter. They are both very badly and shabbily dressed as Cavaliers. All in all they are miserable objects.*

TARVER: Oh don't reproach us, Miss Jedd. It isn't our fault that the Military were summoned to St. Marvells.

DARBEY: You don't blame officers and gentlemen for responding to the sacred call of duty, do you?

SHEBA: No, we blame officers for subjecting two motherless girls to the shock of alighting at the Durnstone Athenaeum to find a notice on the front door: 'Ball knocked on the head – Vivat Regina'.

SALOME: We blame gentlemen for inflicting on us the unspeakable agony of being jeered at by boys.

TARVER: We took the name and address of the child who suggested we call again on the fifth of November. It is on the back of my ticket.

DARBEY: Let me assure you, we shall both wait on his mother for an explanation.

TARVER: Oh, smile on us once again, Miss Jedd – a forced, hollow smile if you will – only smile. Salome!

DARBEY: Sheba!

> *GEORGIANA and SIR TRISTRAM enter.*

GEORGIANA: Salome! Sheba!

SALOME & SHEBA: Aunt!

GEORGIANA: You bad girls!

SALOME: *(Weeping.)* No, Aunt, no!

SHEBA: Not bad, Aunt – trustful and confiding.

GEORGIANA: *(Advancing on TARVER.)* How dare you encourage these two children to enjoy themselves? How dare you take them out without their Aunt? *(Shaking TARVER.)* I'm speaking to you, Field Marshal!

TARVER: Madam, we are on duty.

DARBEY: On heavy duty.

TARVER: We are guarding the ruins of The Swan Inn. You mustn't distract our attention.

GEORGIANA: Guarding the ruins of The Swan Inn, are you? Tris, I may be a feeble woman, but I've a keen sense of right and wrong. Run these outsiders into the road, and let them guard their own ruins.

SALOME and SHEBA shriek and throw themselves at the feet of TARVER and DARBEY, clinging to their legs.

SALOME: No, no! Spare him!

SHEBA: You shall not harm a hair of their heads!

In the struggle, SIR TRISTRAM twists TARVER's wig round so that it covers his face. The gate-bell is heard ringing violently.

LADIES: What's that?

SALOME: It will wake Papa!

SHEBA: Stop the bell!

GEORGIANA runs to the curtains and opens them.

SALOME: *(To TARVER and DARBEY.)* Fly!

SHEBA: Fly!

TARVER and DARBER disappear into the night.

(Falling into SALOME's arms.) We have saved them!

HATCHAM, carrying the basin with the bolus, runs in breathlessly. BLORE enters from the hall, in his dressing gown and carrying his lantern.

GEORGIANA: Oh Tris, your man from the stable!

SIR TRISTRAM: Hatcham!

HATCHAM: Oh, Sir Tristram!

GEORGIANA & SIR TRISTRAM: What is it, Hatcham?

BLORE: What's happened?

HATCHAM: The villain that set fire to The Swan, sir – caught in the act of administering a dose to the horse!

GEORGIANA: Nobbling my Dandy?

SIR TRISTRAM: Where is the scoundrel?

HATCHAM: Topping the Constable's collared him, sir – he's taken him in a cart to the lock-up!

GEORGIANA & SIR TRISTRAM: Oh!

BLORE: *(In agony, aside.)* They've got the Dean!

Thunder and lightning. The curtain falls.

ACT TWO

SCENE ONE

St Marvells police station, the next morning. It is a quaint old room with plaster walls, oak beams and a gothic mullioned window looking onto the street. A massive door, with a small sliding wicket and an iron grating, opens to a prisoner's cell. Other doors lead to the street and to other rooms. This room is partly furnished as a kitchen, partly as a police station (with a small waiting area.), a copy of the Police Regulations and other official documents and implements hanging on the wall.

HANNAH, a buxom, fresh-looking young woman, in a print gown, has been engaged in cooking while singing gaily.

HANNAH: *(Opening a door and calling with a slight dialect.)* Noah, darlin'!

NOAH: *(From another room – in a rough, country voice.)* Yaas!

HANNAH: You'll have your dinner before you drive your prisoner over to Durnstone, won't ye, darlin'?

NOAH: Yaas!

HANNAH: *(Closing the door.)* 'Yaas'! Noah's in a nice temper today over summat. Ah well, I suppose all public figures is liable to irritation.

There is a knock on the outer door. HANNAH, opening it, sees BLORE with a troubled look on his face.

Well I never! Mr Blore from the Deanery! Come in! You might knock me down with a feather!

BLORE: *(Entering and shaking hands mournfully.)* How do you do, Mrs Topping?

HANNAH: And how is the dear Dean, bless him; the sweetest soul in the world?

BLORE: *(Aside.)* Good gracious! She doesn't know of our misfortune. *(To HANNAH.)* I – I haven't seen him this morning!

HANNAH: Well, this is real kind of you, calling on an old friend, Mr Blore. When I think that I were cook at the Deanery seven years, and that since I left you to get wedded not a soul of you has been nigh me, it do seem hard.

BLORE: Well, you see, Hannah, the kitchen took umbrage at your marrying a policeman at Durnstone. It was regarded as a misalliance.

HANNAH: And now Mr Topping's got the appointment of Head Constable at St. Marvells, what's that regarded as?

BLORE: A rise on the scales, Hannah, a decided rise – but still you've only been a week in St. Marvells, and you've got to fight your way up.

HANNAH: I think I'm as up as ever I'm like to be.

BLORE: *(Kissing her cheek.)* And how are you, my dear?

HANNAH: Don't, Edward Blore!

BLORE: 'Don't'? When you was Miss Evans there wasn't these social barriers, Hannah!

HANNAH: Shhh! Noah's jealous of the very apron strings what go round my waist. I'm not so free and handy with my kisses now, I can tell you.

BLORE: But Mr Topping isn't indoors now, surely?

HANNAH: *(Gesturing with her head and pretending to sing to herself.)* La, la, la!

BLORE: Why, he took a man up last night.

HANNAH: What of it?

BLORE: I thought that when any arrest was made in St. Marvells, the prisoner was lodged here only for the night and that the Head Constable had to drive him over to Durnstone Police Station first thing in the morning.

HANNAH: That's the rule, but Noah's behindhand today, and ain't going into Durnstone till after dinner.

BLORE: Then the prisoner is now on the premises!

HANNAH: Yes, he's in our cell. BLORE: Ah! And where is the apartment in question?

HANNAH: The cell? That's it!

BLORE: *(Looking round in horror.)* Oh!

HANNAH: 'The Strong Box' they call it in St. Marvells.

BLORE: Oh, my goodness, only fancy! *(Aside.)* And him accustomed to his shaving water at eight and my kindly hand to button his gaiters. Oh, here's a warning!

HANNAH: Whatever is the matter with you, Mr Blore?

BLORE: Hannah, Hannah my dear, it's this very prisoner what I have called on you respecting.

HANNAH: Oh, so the honour ain't a compliment to me, after all.

BLORE: I'm killing two birds with one stone. But Hannah deary, do you know that this unfortunate man was took in our stables last night.

HANNAH: No, I never ask Noah nothing about the Queen's business. He don't want *two* women over him.

BLORE: Then you haven't seen the miserable culprit?

HANNAH: Lord no. I was in bed hours when Noah brought him home. I take no interest in it at all. They tell us it's only a wretched poacher or a petty larceny we'll get in St. Marvellls. My poor Noah ain't never likely to get the chance of a really big crime in a place what returns a Conservative. My joint's burning. *(She kneels to look into the oven.)*

BLORE: But Hannah, suppose this case you've got hold of now is a case what'll shake old England to its basis! Suppose it means columns in the paper with Topping's name a-figuring!

HANNAH: Hullo! You know something about this arrest, you do!

BLORE: No, no, I don't! I merely said suppose.

HANNAH sits at the table and refers to an official book.

(Aside.) If I could only find out whether Dandy Dick had any of the medicine, it would so guide me at the races. What am I to do? *(To HANNAH.)* It doesn't appear that the horse in the stables – took it, does it?

HANNAH: *(Sharply.)* Took what?

BLORE: Er – took fright. *(Bending over her to look at the records.)* You're sure there's no confession of any sort, Hannah dear?

HANNAH: *(Reading the details.)* The accused was found trespassing in the Deanery stables with intent – refuses to give his name or any account of himself.

NOAH TOPPING appears. He is an uncouth yokel, with red hair, a bristling beard and a vindictive leer. He is dressed in the ill-fitting uniform of a rural police constable.

NOAH: *(Fiercely.)* Hannah!

HANNAH: *(Starting and replacing the book.)* Oh don't! This is Mr Blore from the Deanery come to see us – an old friend of mine!

NOAH: *(Taking BLORE's hand and grasping it firmly.)* A friend of hers is a friend of mine!

BLORE: I hope so, Mr Topping. I thank you.

NOAH: She's getting me a lot of nice new friends this week, since we come to St. Marvells.

BLORE: Of course, dear Hannah was a loving favourite with everybody.

NOAH: Ay. Well then, as *her* friends be *my* friends, I'm taking the liberty of gradually dropping in on 'em all, one by one!

BLORE: *(Extricating his hand.)* Dear me!

NOAH: And if I catch any old fly a-buzzing round my good lady I'll venture to break his head in with my staff!

HANNAH: Oh, Noah!

BLORE: *(Preparing to depart.)* I – I merely called to know if anything had been found out about the ruffian took in our stables last night!

NOAH: Is that *your* business?

BLORE: It – it's my *master's* business.

NOAH: He's the Dean, ain't he?

HANNAH: Yes, Noah, of course.

NOAH: *(Fiercely.)* Shut up, darlin'. Very well then – give Mr Topping's respects to the Dean, and say I'll run up to the Deanery and see him after I've took my man over to Durnstone.

BLORE: Thank you – I hope the Dean will be at home. Good day, Hannah. Good day, Mr Topping.

He offers his hand, into which NOAH significantly places his truncheon. BLORE goes out quickly.

HANNAH: *(Whimpering.)* Oh, Noah, Noah, I don't believe as we shall ever get a large circle of friends round us!

NOAH: Now then. *(Selecting a pair of handcuffs and examining them critically.)* Them'll do. *(Slipping them into his pocket and turning on HANNAH suddenly.)* Hannah!

HANNAH: Yes, Noahry –

NOAH: Add some sparkle, my darlin', to the little time you have me at home with you.

HANNAH: Yes, Noahry. *(She bustles about and begins to lay the table.)*

NOAH: I'm just a-going round to put Samson in the cart.

HANNAH: Oh, don't ye trust to Samson, Noah dear – he's such a vicious brute. Kitty's safer in the cart.

NOAH: Shut up, darling. Samson can take me onto the edge of the hill in half the time.

HANNAH: The hill?

NOAH: Why d'ye think I've put off taking my man to Durnstone till now? Why, I'm a-going to get a glimpse of the racing on my way over. *(Opening the wicket in the cell door and looking in.)* There he is! Sulky! *(To HANNAH.)* Open the oven door, Hannah, and let the smell of the cooking get into him.

HANNAH: Oh no, Noah – that's torture!

NOAH: Do as I tell ye woman! *(She opens the oven door.)* 'Torture'! Of course it's torture! That's my rule! Whenever I get hold of a darned obstinate creature what won't reveal his identity I opens the oven door! Ha! ha! ha!

He goes out into the street, laughing to himself, and, as he departs, the woeful face of THE DEAN appears at the wicket, his head still enveloped in the fur cap.

HANNAH: *(Shutting the oven door.)* Not me! Torturing prisoners might have done for them Middling Ages what Noah's always chattering about, but not for my time of life. I'll shut that wicket. *(Crossing to the door, her face almost comes up against THE DEAN's. She gives a cry.)* The Dean!

THE DEAN: Oh! *(He disappears.)*

HANNAH: Not my old master! Never the master! *(Looking in.)* Master! Look at me! It's Hannah, your poor faithful servant, Hannah!

THE DEAN's face reappears.

THE DEAN: Hannah Evans.

HANNAH: It's Hannah Topping, nee Evans, wife of the Constable what's going to take you to cruel Durnstone.

(Sinking upon the ground at the door, and weeping.) Oh, Mr Dean, sir, what have you been up to? What have you been up to? What *have* you been up to?

THE DEAN: Woman, I am the victim of a misfortune only partially merited.

HANNAH: *(On her knees, clasping her hands.)* Tell me what you've done, Master dear; give it a name, for the love of goodness!

THE DEAN: My poor Hannah, I fear I have placed myself in an equivocal position.

HANNAH: *(With a shriek of despair.)* Agh!

THE DEAN: Be quiet, woman!

HANNAH: Is it a change of cooking that's brought you to such ways? I cooked for you for seven happy years!

THE DEAN: *(Sniffing.)* Alas, you seem to have lost none of your culinary skill!

HANNAH: Master, are you hungry?

THE DEAN: I am sorely tried by your domestic preparations.

HANNAH: *(With a determined look.)* Oh! *(Quickly bolting the street door.)* Noah can't tether that brute of a horse in under ten minutes. *(Producing a large key with which she unlocks the cell door.)* The duplicate key of the Strong Box! Master, you'll give me your word not to cut, won't you?

THE DEAN: Under any other circumstances, Hannah, I should resent that insinuation.

HANNAH: Don't resent nothing! Shove! Shove your hardest, Dean dear!

She pulls the door, which opens sufficiently to let out THE DEAN.

THE DEAN: *(Shaking hands with her as he enters the room.)* Good day, Hannah; you have bettered yourself, I hope?

HANNAH: *(Hysterically flinging herself on THE DEAN.)* Oh, Master, Master!

THE DEAN: *(Forcing her from him sternly.)* Mrs Topping!

HANNAH: Oh, I know, I know, but crime levels all, dear sir!

THE DEAN: You appear to misapprehend the precise degree of criminality which attaches to me. In the eyes of that majestic but imperfect instrument, The Law, I am an innocent if not an injured man.

HANNAH: Stick to that, sir! Stick to it, if you think it's likely to serve your wicked ends!

She places bread and other items on the table.

THE DEAN: My good woman, a single word from me to those at the Deanery would instantly restore me to home, family and accustomed diet.

HANNAH: Ah, they all tell that tale what comes here! So why *don't* you send word, Dean dear?

THE DEAN: Because it would involve revelations of my temporary moral aberration!

HANNAH dissolves into tears once more.

Because I should return to the Deanery with my dignity – that priceless possession of man's middle age! – with my dignity seriously impaired.

HANNAH: *(In despair.)* Oh don't sir, don't!

THE DEAN: How could I face my simple children, who have hitherto, not unreasonably, regarded me as faultless? How could I again walk erect in the streets of St. Marvells with my name blazoned on the records of a police station of the very humblest description?

He sinks into a chair and snatches up a piece of bread.

HANNAH: *(Wiping her eyes.)* Oh sir, it's a treat to hear you, compared with the ordinary criminal class. But listen! I was well fed and kept seven years at the Deanery – I've been wed to Noah Topping eight weeks – that's six years and ten months' loving duty due to you and yours before I owe anything to my darling Noah. Master dear, you shan't be took to Durnstone!

THE DEAN: Silence! Hannah Topping, *née* Evans, it is my duty to inform you that your reasoning does more credit to your heart than to your head.

HANNAH: I can't help it. *(Taking a small key from the table drawer, and putting it in his coat pocket.)* Here, take that! When you once get free from my darling Noah, that key unlocks your handcuffs!

THE DEAN: Handcuffs?

HANNAH: How are you to get free, that's the question now, isn't it? I'll tell you. My Noah will drive you over to Durnstone with old Samson in the cart.

THE DEAN: Old Samson?

HANNAH: That's the horse. Now Samson was formerly in the Durnstone Fire Brigade, and when he hears the familiar signal of a double whistle you can't hold him. *(Putting a whistle into THE DEAN's pocket.)* There's the whistle. Directly you turn into Pear Tree Lane, blow once and you'll see Noah with his nose in the air, pulling fit to wrench his hands off. Jump out – roll clear of the wheels – keep cool and hopeful, and blow again. Before you can get the mud out of your eyes, Noah and the horse and cart will be well into Durnstone, and may Providence restore a young husband safe to his doting wife!

THE DEAN: *(Outraged.)* Hannah, how dare you?

HANNAH turns to him in amazement.

Is this the fruit of your seven years constant cookery at the Deanery?

HANNAH: I wouldn't have suggested it, only this is your first offence.

THE DEAN: *(Aside.)* My 'first offence'!

HANNAH: You're not too old; I want to give you another start in life!

THE DEAN: Another start? Woman, do you think I've no conscience? Do you think I don't realise the enormity of the – of the difficulty of alighting from a vehicle in rapid motion?

HANNAH opens the oven and takes out a small joint in a baking tin, and places it on the table.

HANNAH: It's hunger what's holding you back!

THE DEAN: *(Waving her away.)* I have done with you!

HANNAH: With me, sir – but not with the joint! You'll feel braver when you've had a little nourishment. *(He looks hungrily at the dish.)* That's right, Dean, dear – taste my darling Noah's favourite dish.

THE DEAN: *(Advancing towards the table.)* Oh, Hannah Topping – Hannah Topping! *(Clutching the carving knife despairingly.)* I'll have no more female cooks at the Deanery! This reads me a lesson. *(He starts to carve.)*

HANNAH: Don't stint yourself, sir. You can't blow this whistle on an empty stomach. *(THE DEAN begins to eat.)* Don't my cooking carry you back, sir? Oh, say it do!

THE DEAN: *(With his mouth full.)* It does! It does!

NOAH, unperceived by HANNAH and THE DEAN, climbs in through the window, his eyes wide with rage. He glares round the room, taking everything in at a glance.

NOAH: *(Aside.)* The man of mystery – waited on by my newly-made wife – eating of my favourite meal.

He places his hand on HANNAH's arm. She turns to face him, speechless with fright. THE DEAN continues to eat. HANNAH tries to speak, then clasps her hands and sinks on her knees to NOAH.

THE DEAN: Hannah, a little plain water in a simple tumbler, please.

NOAH: *(Grimly, folding his arms.)* Hannah, introduce me!

HANNAH gives a cry and clings to NOAH's legs.

THE DEAN: *(Calmly to NOAH.)* Am I to gather, constable, from your respective attitudes that you object to these little kindnesses extended to me by your worthy wife?

NOAH: I'm wishing to know the name of my worthy wife's friend. A friend of hers is a friend of mine.

HANNAH: Noahry! Noahry!

NOAH: She's getting me a lot of nice new friends this week since we come to St. Marvells.

HANNAH: Noahry! I made this gentleman's acquaintance through the wicket, in a casual way.

NOAH: Ay. I might have guessed my wedded life would come to this.

HANNAH: He spoke to me just as a strange gentleman ought to speak to a lady! Didn't you, sir – didn't you?

THE DEAN: Hannah, do not let us prevaricate – even under these circumstances. Such is not quite the case! I am no stranger to you.

NOAH advances savagely to THE DEAN. There is a knocking at the door. NOAH restrains himself and faces THE DEAN.

NOAH: No, this is neither the time nor place, with people at the door and dinner on the table, to spill a strange man's blood.

THE DEAN: I trust that your self-respect as an officer of the law will avert anything so unseemly.

NOAH: Ay. That's it! You've touched me on my point of pride. There ain't a police station in all Durnstone conducted more strict and rigid nor what mine is, and so it shall continue. You and me is a-going to set out for Durnstone, and when the charges now standing against you is entered, it's I, Noah Topping, what'll add another!

There is another knock at the door.

HANNAH: Noah!

NOAH: The charge of alienating the affections of my wife, Hannah!

THE DEAN: *(Horrified.)* No, no!

NOAH: Ay, and worse – the embezzling of my midday meal prepared by her hands. *(Pointing to the cell.)* Go in; you have five minutes more in the home you have ruined and laid waste.

THE DEAN: *(Going to the door and turning to NOAH.)* You will at least receive my earnest assurance that this worthy woman is entirely innocent?

NOAH: Innocent? *Innocent?* *(Pointing to the joint on the table.)* Look there! Look there!

THE DEAN, much overcome, disappears through the cell door, which NOAH closes and locks. The knock at the front door is repeated.

Unlock the door, woman!

HANNAH: *(Weeping.)* Oh Noahry, you'll never be popular in St. Marvells.

NOAH: Unlock that door, I say!

HANNAH unlocks the front door, and admits GEORGIANA and SIR TRISTRAM, both dressed for the racecourse.

GEORGIANA: Dear me! Is this the police station?

HANNAH: Yes, lady. Take a chair near the fire. *(To SIR TRISTRAM.)* Sit down, sir.

SIR TRISTRAM: Thank you.

GEORGIANA: This is my first visit to a police station; I hope it will also be my last.

HANNAH: Oh, don't say that, ma'am. We're only auxiliary here, ma'am – the Bench sits at Durnstone.

GEORGIANA: I must say you try to make everybody feel at home.

NOAH has not been noticed and has been surveying GEORGIANA and SIR TRISTRAM.

NOAH: Hannah!

GEORGIANA: Good gracious!

NOAH: Introduce me.

GEORGIANA: What's that? Oh, good morning.

NOAH: Hannah's a-getting me a lot of nice new friends this week since we come to St. Marvells.

HANNAH: Noah, the lady and gentlemen are strangers.

NOAH grunts.

GEORGIANA: Are you the man in charge here?

NOAH: Ay, are you seeing me on business or pleasure?

SIR TRISTRAM: Do you imagine people come here to see *you*?

NOAH: No – they generally come to see my wife. However, if it's business, *(Pointing to the other side of the room.)* that's the official side – this is domestic. You'll all kindly move over.

SIR TRISTRAM & GEORGIANA: *(Changing their seats.)* Oh, certainly.

SIR TRISTRAM: Now, look here my man. This lady is Mrs Tidman. Mrs Tidman is the sister of Dr Jedd, the Dean of St. Marvells.

HANNAH: *(With a gasp.)* Oh!

GEORGIANA: I think there's something wrong with your wife.

NOAH: Ay, there is. She's profligate – proceedings are pending.

GEORGIANA: *(To SIR TRISTRAM.)* What a strange police station.

SIR TRISTRAM: *(To NOAH.)* Well, my good man, to come to the point. My poor friend and this lady's brother, Dr Jedd, the Dean, you know, has mysteriously and unaccountably disappeared.

GEORGIANA: Vanished.

SIR TRISTRAM: Gone.

NOAH: Absconded.

GEORGIANA: Absconded? How dare you!

NOAH: Respectable man, was he?

GEORGIANA: What do you mean?

SIR TRISTRAM: This lady is his sister!

NOAH: Now look here – it's no good a-getting hasty and irritable with the law. I'll come over to you, officially.

Putting the baking tin under his arm he crosses over to SIR TRISTRAM and GEORGIANA.

SIR TRISTRAM: *(Putting his handkerchief to his face.)* Don't bring that horrible odour of cooking over here.

GEORGIANA: Take it away! What is it?

NOAH: It's evidence against my profligate wife.

SIR TRISTRAM and GEORGIANA exchange looks of impatience.

GEORGIANA: Do you realise my poor brother the Dean is missing?

NOAH: Ay – touching this missing Dean.

GEORGIANA: I left him last night to retire to bed.

SIR TRISTRAM: This morning he is not to be found!

NOAH: Ay. Has it struck you to look in his bed?

GEORGIANA & SIR TRISTRAM: Of course!

GEORGIANA: Everybody did that!

NOAH: One would have done. Had he anything on his mind? Money matters p'rhaps?

GEORGIANA: *(Putting her handkerchief to her eyes.)* Yes!

NOAH: Then I've got a theory.

SIR TRISTRAM & GEORGIANA: What is it?

NOAH: A theory that will put you all out of suspense!

SIR TRISTRAM & GEORGIANA: Yes, yes!

NOAH: I've been about a good bit, I read a deal, and I'm a shrewd, experienced man. I should say this is nothing but an ordinary case of suicide.

GEORGIANA & SIR TRISTRAM: For heaven's sake!

GEORGIANA: If this were true how could we break it to the girls?

NOAH: *I* could run up and break it to them if you like.

SIR TRISTRAM: Look here, all *you've* got to do is to hold your tongue and take down my description of the Dean and report his disappearance at Durnstone. *(Pushing him into a chair.)* Go on! *(Dictating.)* 'Missing. The Very Reverend Augustin Jedd, Dean of St. Marvells.' Poor Gus! Poor Gus!

NOAH prepares to write, depositing the baking tin on the table. He writes laboriously, with his legs curled round the chair and his head on the table.

HANNAH: *(Softly to GEORGIANA.)* Lady, lady!

GEORGIANA: *(To HANNAH.)* Eh?

HANNAH: Hush! Listen to me!

She whispers urgently to GEORGIANA.

SIR TRISTRAM: *(Recapping.)* 'The Very Reverend Augustin Jedd, Dean of St. Marvells.' Have you got that?

NOAH: Ay. I'm spelling it my own way.

SIR TRISTRAM: Poor dear old Gus! *(Dictating again.)* 'Description . . .'.

NOAH: *(Unwilling to try writing any more.)* What?

SIR TRISTRAM: 'Description!'

NOAH: I daresay he was just an ordinary looking sort of man.

SIR TRISTRAM: No, no, no! 'Description!'

GEORGIANA: *(Turning from HANNAH, desperately.)* 'Description: a little, short, fat man, with black hair and a squint!'

SIR TRISTRAM: No he isn't.

GEORGIANA: Yes he is.

SIR TRISTRAM: What are you talking about?

GEORGIANA: *I'm* Gus's sister – I ought to know what he looks like!

SIR TRISTRAM: Good heavens, Georgiana – your mind is not going?

GEORGIANA: *(Clutching SIR TRISTRAM's arm and whispering in his ear, as she points to the cell door.)* He's in there!

SIR TRISTRAM: Eh?

GEORGIANA: Gus is the villain they found dosing Dandy Dick last night!

SIR TRISTRAM: *What?*

HANNAH: It's true, sir, he's in there.

SIR TRISTRAM: Good lord! *(To NOAH.)* What have you written?

NOAH: 'Answers to the name of Gus.'

GEORGIANA: *(Snatching the paper from him.)* It doesn't matter. I've changed my mind. I'm too busy to bother about him this week.

NOAH: What? After wasting my time?

GEORGIANA: Look here – you're the constable who took the man in the Deanery stables last night?

NOAH: Ay. My cart's outside, ready to take the scoundrel over to Durnstone.

GEORGIANA: I should like to see him.

NOAH: You can view him passing through. *(He tucks the baking tin under his arm and goes up to the cell door, which he unlocks.)* I warn you – he's an awful looking creature.

GEORGIANA: I can stand it. *(NOAH goes into the cell, closing the door after him.) (To SIR TRISTRAM.)* What was my brother's motive for drugging Dandy last night?

SIR TRISTRAM: I can't think. The first thing to do is to get him out of this hole. This good woman has arranged for his escape.

GEORGIANA: But we can't trust to Gus jumping out of a flying dogcart! Why, it's as much as *I* could do!

HANNAH: Oh no, lady, he'll do it. I've provided for everything. Don't betray him to Noah! There's another – an awfuller – charge hanging over his reverend head.

SIR TRISTRAM: *Another* charge?

GEORGIANA: *Another*? Oh Tris! To think my own stock should run vicious like this.

HANNAH: Hush, lady!

NOAH comes out of the cell with THE DEAN, who is now handcuffed.

GEORGIANA & SIR TRISTRAM: Oh!

THE DEAN raises his eyes and sees SIR TRISTRAM and GEORGIANA. He recoils with a groan, sinking onto a chair.

THE DEAN: Oh!

NOAH: Up you get!

SIR TRISTRAM: No, no – stay! I am the owner of the horse stabled at the Deanery. I make no charge against this wretched person. *(To THE DEAN.)* Oh man, man!

THE DEAN: I was discovered administering to a suffering beast a simple remedy for chills. I am an unfortunate creature. Do with me what you will.

SIR TRISTRAM: *(To NOAH.)* Release this man!

NOAH: Release him? He was found trespassing in the stables of the late Dean, who has committed suicide.

THE DEAN: But *I'm* –

SIR TRISTRAM, GEORGIANA & HANNAH: Hush!

NOAH: The deceased Dean is the only man what can withdraw one charge –

THE DEAN: But *I'm* –

SIR TRISTRAM, GEORGIANA & HANNAH: Hush!

NOAH: And I'm the only man what can withdraw the other.

SIR TRISTRAM: You? Nonsense!

GEORGIANA: Nonsense!

NOAH: I charge this person unknown with alienating the affections of my wife while I was putting my horse to. And I'm going to drive him over to Durnstone with the evidence. *(He brandishes the baking tin and exits.)*

GEORGIANA: It can't be true.

HANNAH: Oh lady, lady, it's appearances what is against us.

NOAH: *(Appearing in the doorway, clutching the horse's reins.)* Whoa! Steady there! Get back! *(We hear the sound – and see the shadow – of a horse rearing up and neighing loudly. NOAH is pulled back into the street. HANNAH shuts the door.)*

GEORGIANA: *(To THE DEAN, severely.)* I am disappointed in you, Augustin. *(Urgently.)* Have you got this wretched woman's whistle?

THE DEAN: Yes.

SIR TRISTRAM: *(To THE DEAN, severely.)* Oh Jedd, Jedd – and these are what you call principles! *(Urgently.)* Have you got the key of your handcuffs?

THE DEAN: Yes.

NOAH: *(Appearing in the doorway.)* Time's up. Come on!

THE DEAN: May I say a few parting words in the home I have apparently wrecked?

NOAH: Say 'em and 'ave done.

THE DEAN: In setting out upon this journey – the termination of which may well be problematical – I desire to attest that this erring constable is the husband of a wife from whom it is impossible to withhold respect, if not admiration.

NOAH: You hear him! Has he no shame?

THE DEAN: As for my wretched self, the confession of my weaknesses must be reserved for another time – another place. *(To GEORGIANA.)* To you, whose privilege it is to shelter in the sanctity of the Deanery, I give this earnest admonition. Within an hour from this terrible moment, let the fire be lighted in the drawing room – let the missing man's warm bath be waiting for its master – a change of linen prepared.

NOAH: This is none of your business. Come away.

THE DEAN: I am ready. Lead me on!

NOAH takes him by the arm and leads him out.

GEORGIANA: Oh, what am I to think of my brother?

HANNAH: It's I and my whistle and Samson the fire-brigade horse what'll bring him back to the Deanery safe and unharmed. Not a soul but we three'll ever know of his misfortune. *(Listening.)* Hark! They're off!

NOAH: *(Outside in the street.)* Get up, now! Get up, old girl!

HANNAH: 'Old girl?' Agh! *(Rushing to the window and looking out.)* He's done for!

GEORGIANA & SIR TRISTRAM: Done for?

HANNAH: The Dean can whistle himself blue! Noah's put Kitty in the cart and left old Samson at home!

HANNAH & GEORGIANA & SIR TRISTRAM: Ah!

Blackout.

SCENE TWO

The morning room at the Deanery, late afternoon on the same day. SALOME and SHEBA are sitting, staring gloomily into space, much as we first saw them in Act I.

SALOME: Poor Papa!

SHEBA: Poor dear Papa!

SALOME: He must return soon – he must!

SHEBA: He *must*! In the meantime, it is such a comfort to feel that we have no cause for self-reproach.

SALOME: But the anxiety is terribly wearing.

SHEBA: Nothing is so weakening, Salome. If I should pine away and ultimately die of this suspense, I want you to have my workbox.

SALOME: *(Shaking her head and turning sadly away.)* Thank you, dear, but if Papa is not home for afternoon tea you will outlive me.

MAJOR TARVER and MR DARBEY appear outside the window.

TARVER: Miss Jedd!

DARBEY: Miss Jedd!

SALOME: Sheba! Here are Gerald Tarver and Mr Darbey!

SHEBA: Oh, the presumption! Open the window and dare them to enter!

SALOME unfastens the French windows, and admits TARVER and DARBEY.

DARBEY: Thank you!

TARVER: Thank you!

SALOME: You do well, gentlemen, to intrude upon two feeble women at a moment of sorrow.

SHEBA: One step further, and I shall ask Major Tarver, who is nearest the bell, to ring for help.

TARVER: Salome – I have loved you distractedly for upwards of eight weeks.

DARBEY: Sheba – Major Tarver loves with a passion second only to my own.

SHEBA: Spare me this scene, Mr Darbey. I have never thought seriously of marriage.

DARBEY: People never do till after they are married.

SHEBA: But think, only think of my age.

DARBEY: Pardon me, Sheba – but what is your age?

SHEBA: Oh, it is so very little – it not worth mentioning. Cannot we remain friends and occasionally correspond?

DARBEY: Well, of course – if you insist –

SHEBA: No, no, I see that is impracticable. It must be wed or part. All I ask is time – time to ponder over such a question. Time to know myself better.

DARBEY: Certainly. How long?

SHEBA: Give me two or three minutes. *(She wanders into the library to ponder.)*

TARVER: Salome – you know the strength of my feelings for you. When can I see the Dean?

SALOME: *(Breaking down.)* Oh, don't, Major!

TARVER: Salome!

SALOME: Papa has been out all night.

DARBEY & TARVER: All night?

SALOME: Isn't it terrible? Oh, what do you think of it, Mr Darbey?

DARBEY: Shocking, but we oughtn't to condemn him unheard.

SALOME: Condemn Papa? What are you talking about? *(Seeing GEORGIANA approaching through the garden.)* Here's Aunt Georgiana!

DARBEY: Eh? Look out, Tarver. *(He exits quickly.)*

SALOME: *(Pulling TARVER after her.)* Come this way and let us take cuttings in the conservatory. *(They go out into the hall.)*

SHEBA: Mr Darbey! Mr Darbey, wait for me! I have decided: Yes! *(She follows the others into the hall as GEORGIANA enters excitedly from the garden.)*

GEORGIANA: *(Waving her handkerchief.)* Come on, Tris! The course is clear! Mind the gatepost! Hold him up! Now give him his head!

SIR TRISTRAM and HATCHAM enter by the window carrying THE DEAN. They all look as though they have recently been engaged in a prolonged struggle.

SIR TRISTRAM: Put him down!

GEORGIANA: Put him down!

HATCHAM: That I will ma'am, and gladly.

They deposit THE DEAN in a chair, and GEORGIANA and SIR TRISTRAM each seize a hand, feeling THE DEAN's pulse.

THE DEAN: *(Opening his eyes.)* Where am I now?

GEORGIANA: He lives! Hurrah! Cheer man, cheer!

HATCHAM: Hurrah!

SIR TRISTRAM: We can't shout here; you can go and cheer as loudly as you like in the roadway by yourself.

HATCHAM: Yes, sir. *(He runs out into the garden.)* Hurrah!

THE DEAN: *(Gradually recovering.)* Georgiana – Mardon.

SIR TRISTRAM: How are you, Jedd, old boy?

GEORGIANA: How do you feel now, Gus?

THE DEAN: Torn to fragments.

SIR TRISTRAM: So you are. *(To GEORGIANA.)* Thank heavens, he's conscious!

THE DEAN: I feel as if I had been walked over carefully by a large concourse of the lower orders.

GEORGIANA: So you have been. *(To SIR TRISTRAM.)* Thank heavens, his memory is all right.

THE DEAN: Do I understand that I have been forcibly and illegally rescued?

SIR TRISTRAM: That's it, old fellow.

THE DEAN: Who has committed such a reprehensible act?

SIR TRISTRAM: A woman who would have been a heroine in any age – Georgiana!

THE DEAN: Georgiana, I am bound to overlook it in a relative, but never let this occur again.

SIR TRISTRAM: Tell him what happened.

GEORGIANA: You found out that that other woman's plan went lame, didn't you?

THE DEAN: I discovered its limitations after a prolonged period of ineffectual whistling.

GEORGIANA: But we ascertained the road that the genial constable was going to follow. He was bound for the edge of the hill, up Pear Tree Lane, to watch the races. Directly we knew this, Tris and I made for the hill. Bless your soul, there were hundreds of my old friends there – welshers, pickpockets, cardsharpers, all the lowest racecourse cads in the kingdom. In a minute I was in the middle of 'em, as much at home as a duchess in a drawing room.

SIR TRISTRAM: A queen in a palace!

GEORGIANA: Boadicea among the Druids! 'Do you know me?' I holloaed out. Instantly there was a cry of 'Blessed if it ain't Gorge Tidd!' Tears of real joy sprang to my eyes; while I was wiping them away, Tris had his pockets emptied and I lost my watch.

SIR TRISTRAM: Ah, Jedd, it was a glorious moment!

GEORGIANA: 'Dear friends', I said; 'Brothers! I'm with you once again.' You should have heard the shouts of honest welcome. 'Listen to me,' I said. 'A very dear relative of mine has been collared for playing the three-card trick on his way down from Town.' There was a groan of sympathy. 'He'll be on the brow of the hill with a bobby in half an hour,' said I. 'Who's for the rescue?' A dead deep silence followed, broken only by the sweet voice of a young child asking 'What'll we get for it?' 'A pound a-piece,' said I. There was a roar of assent, and my concluding words, 'and possibly six months', were never heard. *(Seizing THE DEAN by the hand and dragging him up.)* So now you know whose hands have led you back to your own manger. *(Embracing him.)* And oh, brother, confess – isn't there something good and noble in true English sport after all?

THE DEAN: Every abused institution has its redeeming characteristic. But whence is the money to come to reward these dreadful persons? I cannot reasonably ask my girls to organise a bazaar or concert.

GEORGIANA: Concert? I'm a rich woman!

THE DEAN: Are you?

GEORGIANA: Well, I've cleared fifteen hundred over the Handicap.

THE DEAN: No! Then the horse who enjoyed the shelter of the Deanery last night –

SIR TRISTRAM: Dandy Dick –

THE DEAN: Won!

GEORGIANA: In a common canter! All the rest nowhere – including –

GEORGIANA & SIR TRISTRAM: Bonny Betsy!

THE DEAN: *(Aside.)* Five hundred pounds towards the spire! Five hundred! Oh, where is Blore with the good news?

SIR TRISTRAM: *(To GEORGIANA.)* Look at him! Lively as a cricket!

THE DEAN: Sir Tristram, I am under the impression that your horse reluctantly swallowed a small portion of the bolus last night before I was surprised and removed.

SIR TRISTRAM: By-the-bye, I am expecting the analysis of that concoction every minute.

THE DEAN: Spare yourself the trouble – the secret is mine. I seek no acknowledgement from either of you, but in your moment of deplorable triumph, remember with gratitude a slim volume entitled *The Horse and Its Ailments*, and the prosaic name of its humane author – John Cox. *(He goes out through the library.)*

GEORGIANA: But oh, Tris Mardon, what can I ever say to you?

SIR TRISTRAM: Anything you like except 'Thank you'!

GEORGIANA: Don't stop me! Why, you were the man who hauled Augustin out of the cart by his legs!

SIR TRISTRAM: Oh, but why mention such trifles?

GEORGIANA: They're not trifles. And when his cap fell off, it was you – brave fellow that you are – who pulled the horse's nosebag over my brother's head so that he shouldn't be recognised.

SIR TRISTRAM: My dear Georgiana, these are the common courtesies of everyday life.

GEORGIANA: They are acts that any true woman would esteem. Gus won't readily forget the critical moment when all the cut chaff ran down the back of his neck – nor shall I.

SIR TRISTRAM: Nor shall *I* forget the way in which you gave Dandy his whisky out of a soda-water bottle just before the race.

GEORGIANA: That's nothing – any lady would have done the same.

SIR TRISTRAM: Nothing? You looked like the Florence Nightingale of the paddock! Oh Georgiana, why, why, why won't you marry me?

GEORGIANA: Why?

SIR TRISTRAM: Why?

GEORGIANA: Why, because you've only just asked me, Tris!

SIR TRISTRAM: But when I touched your hand last night, you reared!

GEORGIANA: Yes, Tris, old man, but love is founded on mutual esteem; last night you hadn't put my brother's head in that nosebag.

Unseen by them, SHEBA looks in at the door.

SHEBA: *(Aside.)* How annoying! There's Aunt and Sir Tristram in this room – Salome and Major Tarver are sitting on the hot pipes in the conservatory – where are Mr Darbey and I to go?

THE DEAN enters through the library carrying a paper in his hand; he has now resumed his normal appearance. SHEBA is astonished to see him.

(Aside.) Papa? Come back? *(She withdraws in great excitement and shuts the door.)*

THE DEAN: *(Aside.)* Home! What sonorous music is in the word! Home, with the secret of my sad misfortune buried in the bosoms of a faithful few. Home, with my family influence intact! Home, with the sceptre of my dignity still tight in my grasp! *(Looking at the paper in his hand.)* What is this that I have picked up on the stairs?

He reads with a horrified look as HATCHAM enters from the garden.

HATCHAM: Beg Pardon, Sir Tristram.

SIR TRISTRAM: What is it?

HATCHAM: The chemist has just brought the analysis.

SIR TRISTRAM: Where is he? Let me see.

SIR TRISTRAM and GEORGIANA go into the garden, following HATCHAM.

THE DEAN: It is too horrible. *(Reading.)* 'Debtor to Lewis Isaacs, *Costumier* to the Queen, Bow Street – Total, forty pounds, nineteen!' There was a fancy dress ball at Durnstone last night! Salome – Sheba – no, no!

SALOME and SHEBA bound in and rush over to THE DEAN.

SALOME & SHEBA: Papa, Papa!

SALOME: Our own Papa!

SHEBA: Papsey!

They embrace him enthusiastically.

SALOME: Our parent returned!

SHEBA: Papsey – come back!

THE DEAN: Stop!

SALOME: Papa, why have you tortured us with anxiety?

SHEBA: Where have you been, you naughty man?

THE DEAN: Before I answer that question, which I can't help feeling, from a child to its parent, smacks of impertinence, I demand an explanation of this disreputable document. *(Reading.)* 'Debtor to Lewis Isaacs, *Costumier* to the Queen.'

SALOME & SHEBA: Oh!

They collapse aghast on the nearest furniture.

THE DEAN: I will not follow this legend in all its revolting intricacies. Suffice it to say, its moral is inculcated by the mournful total. Forty pounds, nineteen! Imps of deceit! *(Looking from one to another.)* There was a ball at Durnstone last night. I know it.

SHEBA: Spare us!

SALOME: You couldn't have been there, Papa!

THE DEAN: Been there? I trust I was better – that is, otherwise employed. *(Referring to the bill.)* Which of my hitherto trusted daughters was a shepherdess – period – late 18th century? *(SHEBA points to SALOME.)* And a flower fairy of an indeterminate epoch? *(SALOME points to SHEBA.)* To your respective rooms! *(The girls cling together.)* Let your blinds be drawn. At seven porridge will be brought to you.

SALOME: Papa!

THE DEAN: Go!

SHEBA: Papsey!

THE DEAN: Go!

SALOME: Papa, poor girls as we are, we can pay the bill.

THE DEAN: You cannot – go!

SHEBA: Through the kindness of our Aunt –

SALOME: We have won fifty pounds.

THE DEAN: What?

SHEBA: At the races!

THE DEAN: *(Recoiling.)* You too! You too drawn into the vortex! Is there no conscience that is clear – is there no guilelessness left in this house, with the possible exception of my own? *(Handing SALOME the bill.)* Take this horrid thing – never let it meet my eyes again. As for the scandalous costumes, they shall be raffled in aid of local charities. Confidence, that precious pearl in the snug shell of domesticity, is at an end between us. I punish you both by permanently withholding from you the reason of my absence from home last night. Go!

The girls file out to the hall as SIR TRISTRAM marches in from the garden, followed by GEORGIANA, who is carrying the basin containing the bolus. SIR TRISTRAM has an opened letter in his hand.

SIR TRISTRAM: Good heavens, Jedd! The analysis has arrived!

THE DEAN: I am absolutely indifferent!

GEORGIANA & SIR TRISTRAM: Indifferent?

THE DEAN: *(To GEORGIANA.)* How dare you confront me without even the semblance of a blush – you who have enabled my innocent babes, for the first time in their lives, to pay one of their own bills.

SHEBA and SALOME creep into the library.

SIR TRISTRAM: Jedd, you were once my friend, and you are to be my relative. But not even our approaching family tie prevents my designating you as one of the most atrocious conspirators known in the history of the Turf.

THE DEAN: Conspirator?

SIR TRISTRAM: As the owner of one half of Dandy Dick, I denounce you!

GEORGIANA: As the owner of the *other* half, *I* denounce you!

THE DEAN: You?

SHEBA and SALOME, unnoticed, listen to all that is said.

SIR TRISTRAM: The chief ingredient of your infernal preparation is known.

THE DEAN: It contains nothing that I would not cheerfully administer to my own children.

GEORGIANA: *(In horror.)* Oh!

SIR TRISTRAM: I believe you! *(Pointing to the paper.)* Strychnine! Sixteen grains!

SALOME & SHEBA: *(Clinging to each other, terrified.)* Oh!

THE DEAN: Strychnine? I will summon my devoted servant Blore, in whose presence the innocuous mixture was compounded.

THE DEAN rings the bell. The girls hide from view.

This analysis is simply the pardonable result of over-enthusiasm on the part of our local chemist.

GEORGIANA: You're a disgrace to the pretty little police station where you slept last night!

BLORE enters and stands unnoticed.

THE DEAN: I will gladly prove that in the Deanery stables the common laws of hospitality have never been transgressed. Give me the bowl! *(GEORGIANA hands him the basin.)* A simple remedy for a chill.

SIR TRISTRAM: Strychnine!

GEORGIANA: Sixteen grains!

THE DEAN: I myself am suffering from the exposure of last night. *(Taking the remaining bolus and opening his mouth.)* Observe me!

He is just about to put the bolus in his mouth when BLORE rushes forward, snatching the basin from his hands.

BLORE: Don't, don't, don't!

THE DEAN: Blore!

BLORE: *(Sinking to his knees.) I* did it! I had an honest fancy for Bonny Betsy, and I wanted Dandy Dick out of the way. And while you was mixing the dose with the best ecclesiastical intentions, I introduced a foreign element.

SIR TRISTRAM: *(Pulling BLORE up by his coat collar.)* Viper!

BLORE: Oh sir, it was all for the sake of the Dean.

SIR TRISTRAM: The Dean?

BLORE: The dear Dean said he only had fifty pounds to spare for sporting purposes, and I thought a gentleman of his high standing ought to have a certainty.

SIR TRISTRAM: Jedd!

GEORGIANA: Augustin!

THE DEAN: I can conceal it no longer. I – I instructed this unworthy creature to back Dandy Dick on behalf of the Restoration Fund.

SIR TRISTRAM: *(Shaking BLORE.)* And didn't you do it?

BLORE: No.

THE DEAN: What? Why not? In the name of that tottering spire, why not?

BLORE: Oh sir, thinking as you'd given some of the mixture to Dandy, I put your cheerful little offering on Bonny Betsy.

THE DEAN: Oh! *(To BLORE.)* I could have pardoned everything but this last act of disobedience. You are unworthy of the Deanery. Leave it for some lesser household.

BLORE: If I leave the Deanery, I shall give my reasons, and then what'll folks think of you and me in our old age?

THE DEAN: You wouldn't spread this tale in St. Marvells?

BLORE: Not if sober, sir – but suppose grief drove me to my cups?

THE DEAN: I must save you from intemperance at any cost. Remain in my service – a sad, sober but, above all, a silent man!

SALOME and SHEBA step forward.

SALOME: Papa!

THE DEAN: Get back to your rooms! I am distracted!

SHEBA: No, no, Papa; we have accidentally discovered that you, our parent, have stooped to deception, if not to crime.

THE DEAN: *(Staggering back.)* Oh!

SHEBA: We are still young – the sooner, therefore, we are removed from any unfortunate influence the better.

SALOME: We have the chance to start a new life. *(Indicating the hall.)* Major Tarver and Mr Darbey have proposed to us.

THE DEAN: Major Tarver and Mr Darbey? Where are they? *(He rushes out, followed by SALOME and SHEBA.)*

As soon as they have disappeared, a dishevelled NOAH TOPPING runs in from the garden with HANNAH clinging to him.

NOAH: *(Glaring round the room.)* Is this here the Deanery?

HANNAH: Noahry, come back!

NOAH: There's been a man rescued from my lawful custody while my face was unofficially held downwards in the mud. The villain has been traced back to the Deanery.

SIR TRISTRAM: Nonsense!

HANNAH: Come away!

NOAH: The man was an unknown lover of my newly-made wife!

GEORGIANA: You mustn't bring your domestic affairs here!

THE DEAN is heard outside.

THE DEAN: Come in, Major Tarver – come in, Mr Darbey!

NOAH: That's his voice!

THE DEAN enters, followed by SALOME, TARVER, SHEBA and DARBEY.

(Confronting THE DEAN.) My man.

GEORGIANA: You're speaking to Dr Jedd, the Dean of St. Marvells.

NOAH: I'm speaking to the man I took last night – the villain who has alienated the affections of my wife.

SIR TRISTRAM: Wait – one moment! *(He goes out into the garden.)*

THE DEAN: *(Mildly.)* Do not let us chide a man who is conscientious even in error. *(Looking at HANNAH.)* I think I see Hannah Evans, once an excellent cook under this very roof.

HANNAH: I'm Mrs Topping now, sir – bride of the constable. And oh, do forgive him – he's a mass of ignorance.

NOAH: Come away!

HANNAH returns to NOAH as SIR TRISTRAM re-enters with HATCHAM.

SIR TRISTRAM: *(To HATCHAM.)* Hatcham *(Pointing to THE DEAN.)* – is that the man you and the constable apprehended in the stables last night?

HATCHAM: That, sir? Bless your heart, sir, that's the Dean himself.

SIR TRISTRAM: That'll do.

HATCHAM: *(To NOAH.)* Why, our man was a short, fat individual.

SIR TRISTRAM: Thank you!

HATCHAM goes back into the garden.

THE DEAN: *(To NOAH.)* I trust you are perfectly satisfied.

NOAH: *(Wiping his brow and looking puzzled.)* I'm done.

THE DEAN: Don't trouble further. I withdraw unreservedly any charge against the unknown person found on my premises last night. I attribute to him the most innocent intentions. Hannah, you and your worthy husband will stay and dine in my kitchen.

NOAH: Is it a hot dinner?

THE DEAN: Hot – with ale.

NOAH: *(To HANNAH.)* Now then, you don't know a real gentleman when you see one. Why don't ye thank the Dean warmly?

HANNAH: *(Kissing THE DEAN's hand with a curtsey.)* Thank you, sir.

THE DEAN: *(Benignly.)* Go – go. I take a kindly interest in you both.

They back out, bowing and curtseying. SHEBA sits at the piano and plays softly, DARBEY at her side.

GEORGIANA: Well, Gus, you're out of all your troubles. Are you happy?

THE DEAN: Happy? My family influence gone forever – my dignity crushed out of all recognition – the genial summer of the Deanery frosted by the winter of Deceit.

GEORGIANA: *(Slapping THE DEAN on the back.)* Look here, Augustin, George Tidd will lend you that thousand for the poor old spire.

THE DEAN: *(Taking her hand.)* Oh, Georgiana!

GEORGIANA: On one condition – that you'll admit there's no harm in our laughter at a Sporting Dean.

THE DEAN: No, no – I cannot allow it!

SIR TRISTRAM: Why, Jedd, there's no harm in laughter, for those who laugh or for those who are laughed at.

GEORGIANA: Provided – firstly, that it is Folly that is mocked and not Virtue; and secondly, that it is our friends who laugh at us *(To the audience.)*, as we hope they all will, for our pains.

Curtain.

.